PROPHET OF PLENTY
The First Ninety Years of W. D. Weatherford

PROPHET OF PLENTY

THE FIRST NINETY YEARS OF

W. D. Weatherford

by Wilma Dykeman

THE UNIVERSITY OF TENNESSEE PRESS   KNOXVILLE

Books by Wilma Dykeman

THE FRENCH BROAD
Rivers of America Series, 1955. New edition, 1965

NEITHER BLACK NOR WHITE
(with James Stokely), 1957

SEEDS OF SOUTHERN CHANGE
(with James Stokely), 1962

THE TALL WOMAN
a novel, 1962

THE FAR FAMILY
a novel, 1966

PROPHET OF PLENTY
THE FIRST NINETY YEARS OF W. D. WEATHERFORD, 1966

Copyright © 1966 by Wilma Dykeman.
All Rights Reserved. Manufactured in the
United States of America. First Edition.
Library of Congress Catalog Card Number: 66-26067

Second Printing, 1967

Prophet of Plenty
is dedicated to today's youth—
tomorrow's leaders—
to whom W. D. Weatherford pledged
his talents, his energy, and the time
of his life

FOREWORD by Terry Sanford

The first time I met W. D. Weatherford, I didn't believe it. I had heard about this scholar of the mountains. I had seen from the highway the stately YMCA Assembly building commanding the valleys from its mountain loft, and recently I had sat on its columned veranda and reflected that this must be the most relaxing, exhilarating, satisfying spot on earth. I knew he had put the Assembly there, and had made it what it was, and that it was an old building. I assumed that he was an old man.

I was emphatically wrong! At our first encounter he was walking down the drive of the Blue Ridge Assembly, his Phi Beta Kappa key swinging with his athletic strides. He grasped my hand and arm, and I felt the presence of energy as you might expect on the fringes of a tornado or in the aftermath of an atomic bomb. He was only eighty or eighty-five or so. This wasn't an old man at all. This was some kind of an angular mountain bear with gentle face and lively eyes, a combination somehow of constrained strength and infinite gentleness.

I wanted to know more about him, and I learned all I could. And now Wilma Dykeman, talented writer, has brought together on these pages a powerful and power-giving biography of this ageless mountain spirit. I am sure Miss Dykeman wasn't ambitious enough to think she could capture his spirit, because he is still galloping on that spirit up and down mountain coves, and across the lives of Appalachia, too fast and furiously for capture. But she has caught the shadows on the mountains, and the reflections on the clouds, as he has moved for ninety years to make his life lift up the lives of all who were fortunate enough to have been in his orbit. Wilma Dykeman has written of those days, and no one can read her account without wishing that as a youth he might have known this man.

For he is no ordinary man. Out of the harsh country just west of Fort Worth, Texas, he came by raw determination to Vanderbilt University. Those who know of Dr. Weatherford as the man who brought the nation's conscience to bear on the problems of the Appalachian mountains may not know that he had already filled an ordinary lifetime with extraordinary accomplishments before he ever began his monumental *Southern Appalachian Region: A Survey.*

He had written some twenty books. He was a successful director of a major business, pioneering profit-sharing and fighting child labor. He was an educator and college professor.

Most important, however, beginning at the turn of the century, he was one of the few prophets of a new and hopeful South when prophets were needed. As International YMCA Secretary for Colleges of the South and Southwest, beginning in 1902, he repeatedly visited every college in the South. Here were fertile fields to be worked. Here were the students, who, he insisted, would begin anew the development of the region by their own individual development.

At the turn of the century Weatherford's region was bogged down in poverty, dominated by Northern high-interest capital, suffering under discriminatory freight rates, plagued by demagogues, and fighting for its life from the depths of the aftermath of so-called Reconstruction.

There was one way up: education for leadership; education for jobs; education for citizenship. This was his message to the youth of the South. This was their land and their excellence would determine its excellence.

The building of regional competence began with the building of individual competence. The answer for a region lay in its people. Dr. Weatherford, always a man of clear vision, saw before most others, some fifty years before it was to become a part of the national understanding and policy, that our human resources are the heart of the nation's hopes. He started with people and he has stayed with people for the two-thirds of this century he has been engaged in building his region.

He wasn't talking about just the young leaders who had managed to find their way to college. He meant all people—the tenant farmer and the mill worker drawing starvation wages, the exploited child, and the Negro. By words and action Dr. Weatherford insisted that the South could not rise with the Negro as a yoke. The Negro could not be carried by the white population. He had to be given the opportunity of education and a fair break for a decent life. These words and actions would have been courageous in the sixties; he was driving headlong at the issue a full decade before World War I.

The traveling and speaking and counseling were not enough. Shortly after he became Secretary, with his own imagination and money raising, he established and built the Blue Ridge Assembly. Here he brought brilliant leaders to meet with thousands of eager students embracing several generations, to stir their resolve, and to send them back for crucial roles in an emerging land.

There is no way to measure this influence of life on life

as the Weatherford ideas of excellence, of self-discipline, of concern for all people, of determination and industry, reached virtually every community of the South, and indeed other parts of the country and as far away as China. He set out to reach his students, to lift up their ambitions, to ennoble their lives, and they in turn have reached out and lifted up, and there is no end.

This story of the gadfly of the South, standing by itself, would have made a story worth telling, and his remarkable career as champion of quality education and fairness to all races would have been a dramatic biography. But this is only part of the story.

His work at Berea College, and his life in the Appalachians at Blue Ridge brought him close to a region in America being bypassed by American progress. From his experiences with these people, there blended and developed a new career, to bring the people of Appalachia back into the mainstream of America.

Again the center of his theme was people. The people of Appalachia, he was the first to say, were the descendants of the sturdiest of the pioneers, those who had pushed west to break the land and draw on its sustenance. Give them the opportunity to develop, and they will develop the region. His emphasis was on individuals, and not one, he felt, could we afford to neglect.

It is probably fair to say that he is the father of the present massive and pioneering efforts to open up the Appalachian country. His work, and his faith, and his idea caught the attention of governmental leaders, and turned the attention of the state and federal governments to this land of opportunity.

Wilma Dykeman recounts vividly his trials, his obstacles, his disappointments, his triumphs, his treks across the South by steam locomotive trains to his trips to the ridges and hollows by his wonderful Jeep, which he is driving to this day.

There is a powerful message in the story of this life. It says to the nation, look to your people and you will grow great. It says to every individual that here is an example of tremendous dedication, of selfless purpose, of constant courage, and clear-eyed vision. It is a story that should have been put down where all can know and draw strength from the example of such a life. No one can read this without trying to make his life count for a little more, without saying what the Weatherfords' then seven-year-old son, in a blessing he had learned from his daddy, startled breakfast guests by saying: "Lord, give us a man's work to do today."

With all of his other achievements, Dr. Weatherford also may very well have found for us the long-sought Fountain of Youth. The Dykeman story of Weatherford is a better guide than the chronicles of Ponce de León. Make your life fiercely dedicated to every human being everywhere; have unfinished business of unreachable goals, and strive every day to reach them; and spare not yourself, as if you had but a day to do it all. It works. He is approaching ninety-one, vigorous, alert, full of energy, concerned and working on his unfinished business.

T. S.

Raleigh, North Carolina

PROPHET OF PLENTY: W. D. Weatherford

1

They said of W. D. Weatherford's mother on the plains of Texas that she got up from her chair running. People who know him say that Willis Duke Weatherford came out of his crib running—and has not slowed down in the ninety years since.

Perhaps Margaret Jane Turner had learned to take long strides while she was growing up in the rugged hills of North Carolina where a pioneer people "made-do or did without." Perhaps her son learned a stiff pace while he was coming of age on a hardscrabble Texas farm in a destitute South. At any rate, this is the story of his attack on poverty wherever he found it. It is also the record of his prophecy of the plenty which was, and is, available to a man or a nation.

"Poverty is fashionable this season," cynics in Washington said during the country's 1965 awakening to the extent of certain urban and rural needs. Many spoke of it. How many understood its reality?

What is poverty?

Let us be very specific and precise. It is of the senses.

Poverty is a smell. It is the cooking smell of old grease used and re-used, saturated into clothes and hair and rotting upholstery; the sleeping smell of beds crowded with ill-nourished bodies, and threadbare blankets soaked with odors of sickness and staleness; the smoking smells of cheap tobacco rolled into brown paper cigarettes, or lumps of grimy coal spreading from grate or cookstove. Gutter-sewers, overripe garbage, dust and heat in summer, cold and permeating dampness in winter. A stifling, nauseating, omnipotent smell.

Poverty is a sound. It is the sound of perpetual crying: an infant mewling, a mother mourning, an old man moaning. The sound is of shrieks in the night, noise the day long. Shuffling feet, hacking coughs, rustling vermin, insistent leaks and drips and crackings. Conflict, disintegration, more deafening in its constancy than its loudness: this is the sound-track of poverty's grind.

Winding down a remote road in East Tennessee's Cumberland Mountains one day not long ago, Weatherford contemplated a valley of miserable shacks with their lonely antennae of quiet desperation and said to a friend, "We hear talk about 'pockets of poverty.' There is no such thing as a pocket of poverty. It cannot be contained. It spreads over the whole fabric of life."

Poverty is a sight. It is the sight of slumped shoulders, useless hands stuffed into empty pockets, averted eyes. The scene is of land ill-used—barren, blasted, junk-strewn wasteland—or of streets that are blighted wildernesses of asphalt, brick, steel, and random-blowing trash. The sight is of faces pinched by years of need, guarded permanently from hope; and it is the raw ugliness of crowded, unscreened, fly-specked rooms, and of faded clothes too large or tight or threadbare for the body they conceal. Glaring, nerve-wracking city lights outside; and inside, the dim, dingy, ceiling bulbs that cast shadows but no illumination. Unrelieved, lifelong ugliness: this is the face of poverty.

When one Kentucky boy came to join the Job Corps sponsored by the federal government, he told his counselor that his mother had advised him to leave home. "And don't come back here, boy. There's nothing here but the graveyard."

Poverty is a feeling—through the pores, in the belly, on the feet. Cold so sharp it burns and heat so sweltering and oppressive it chills with a clammy sweat. The feeling of poverty is dull aches, twinges, pangs, brief satisfactions, creeping numbness. Pain.

Poverty is a taste. It is the taste of hot saliva boiling into the mouth before nausea, of dried beans and chicken gizzards and hog skins and too many starches and too few fruits. Stale bread and spoiling vegetables, cheap coffee and the sweet momentary fizz of soft drinks that allay but do not alleviate hunger pangs. The taste is compounded of snuff, tobacco, decaying teeth, flour gravy, headache powders, raw whiskey, bitterness.

An Appalachian candidate at a Job Corps camp slipped away at mealtime and would not eat. When questioned, he finally admitted that his teeth ached and he was afraid of being expelled if he told anyone. He went for a check-up; the camp dentist pulled fifteen rotten teeth.

This is the poverty of the body.

It gnaws at individuals one by suffering one.

But poverty is more than the sum of its physical parts. It is not only hunger today but fear of tomorrow. Not only present chill but future freeze. Not only daily discomfort but accumulations of illness. It is fear, but fear made impotent by the enormity of today's demands and an insufficiency of energy to forestall tomorrow's defeats.

Poverty is of the mind, too. And its root and flower is apathy. Apathy so total that the body is drained of all but the dullest perception, and the mind is drugged to all but the most primitive hungers. The light of reason—curiosity, search, comparison, logic—flickers feebly.

This is poverty of the mind.

It gnaws at people singly and in groups, stifling them, condemning them to living death.

Then there is poverty of the spirit. This is the darkest, subtlest, most widespread deprivation of all. For this is the poverty that afflicts those who have money as well as those who have none. Its need is deeper than flesh and more craving than thirst. It witnesses tears but does not weep, permits pain and never winces, indulges ignorance without protest, hears cries for help and remains unmoved. It denies the human capacity for empathy and the creative necessity for imagination.

This is poverty of the spirit, malnutrition of vision.

It can destroy civilizations.

These are the poverties that have claimed the lifetime attention of W. D. Weatherford.

Physical poverty has captured our national attention. Books, films, reports in breadth and depth have aroused public awareness of the cancer gnawing at our affluent image. Massive appropriations of money have been mustered to doctor the symptoms and, hopefully, to destroy their festering sources at the roots. Impressive investments of time and energy on the part of many people have been channeled into this assault on a domestic ill. Yet one problem persists: poverty is dreary and daily, and as our initial alarm and surface sympathy grow weary and diminish, how can we sustain a deeper concern among more people? How can we invest our money and our hours, not with dwindling enthusiasm but ever more intelligently and imaginatively? Above all, how can we become involved at the personal level in an attack on all our neglect?

4

One public opinion poll early in 1964 revealed that 51 per cent of our comfortable middle-class Americans believed that the poverty-stricken in our midst could pull out of their deep trouble if only they wanted to.

If the physical and intellectual poverty of some segments of our population reflects a spiritual poverty in all of us, then how—individually and purposefully—may we overcome these poverties with a new plenty?

And what is plenty?

Plenty is sufficiency—food, heat, clothing, shelter, cleanliness—of those things that nourish the body. Plenty is abundance of those riches that feed and stretch the mind: schools, books, travel, music, art, experience, leisure. Plenty is a release of those energies that we call, in the inadequate language of words, moral or spiritual. Plenty is that sufficiency for the body, abundance for the mind, and upthrust of the spirit which can let man fulfill his largest creative capacities.

It is vision of such plenteousness that has propelled W. D. Weatherford through nearly three-quarters of a century of religious, educational, and social pioneering in his native South.

There are few enough people who can see either the poverty or the potential within the eye's reach. As in the fable of the blind Indians and the elephant, in which each man described the strange beast by the single part of its anatomy which he touched (tail, ear, trunk, hide), so most of those looking at poverty today see only that segment which fits their own limited comprehension.

To some extent this is adequate, even necessary. Specialists must focus their microscopic surveys on the causes, the effects, the alleviations of poverty. To the same purpose we must have experts who will use the tools of their knowledge and training. But beyond these we must heed others who are looking at the parts but seeing the whole, working at the small problems but building toward the larger possibilities, who are afraid of neither the drudgery nor the dreams.

Ours is a season when prophets seem indeed to be without honor (or public relations agents) in their own country. Just now it is rather more stylish to compute necessary statistics and to compile case histories than to interpret new ways for understanding and nourishing the human spirit.

It is useful, however, even if somewhat unfashionable, for some of us to confront a man who is such a leader. In an undertaking where bureaus, agencies, committees, even well-intentioned charities, frequently seem to submerge the very people they are meant to rescue, it is worth our while to meet a man who is convinced that person-to-person concern and labor is not only possible but also essential if we are to take any permanent step up from poverty into the freedom of such plenty as we have described.

There are two reasons for this book about W. D. Weatherford. First, as informal history it may help to fill certain gaps in our knowledge of the Southern past. Second, as inspiration it may help to fill some present void of belief in our concept of God and our faith in ourselves. Weatherford's life is not only a record of the past; it is also a catalyst for the future.

This account of Weatherford's work is neither definitive biography nor formal scholarship. Rather it is a record of one man's response to the challenges of his times. Over the span of almost a century those times altered so drastically that, as one of his contemporaries has said, "In my lifetime changes have occurred as dynamic and far-reaching as all others since Homer and Abraham."

When W. D. Weatherford was born, Ulysses S. Grant was President of the United States and Victoria was

Queen of England. Edison's light bulb, Henry Ford's motor car, the Wrights' airplane, Freud's dreams, and Einstein's relativity were not even on the immediate horizon. Most of the population lived in the country; there were calomel and turpentine instead of bufferin and penicillin, and it took Weatherford's father longer to hitch up his wagon and team and drive into the near-by village of Weatherford, Texas, than it takes his son today to jet from his home in the mountains of North Carolina to Washington, D. C. Yes, the times changed— and he changed with them. Sometimes he was ahead of them. It is what he saw, understood, did, *in the context of the decades in which he was working*, that makes Weatherford's story meaningful.

He came out of the Western frontier to pioneer new frontiers. This task required a special sort of character, which was an asset Weatherford had in abundance. As Gerald W. Johnson has written of one of Weatherford's political heroes, Andrew Jackson, so we might say of Weatherford: "It was his fate to live on the frontier, where men were disciplined, indeed, but not with the discipline of settled communities. The discipline of the frontier hardens, but does not bleach."

Proud, persistent, curious, and courageous, Weatherford has exasperated friends, enraged enemies, been the inspiration of youth and the despair of dogma. The fires may have hardened his determination, but they never bleached him into passivity or indifference or dull conformity. "A dedicated bulldozer," one academic acquaintance has called Weatherford, and whether he put the emphasis on the adjective or the noun would mark the division between Weatherford's enthusiastic disciples and his disenchanted dissenters. It is difficult to find many in between.

During the early decades of this century the controversy between theology and science seemed destined to wreck many a distinguished scholarly career and institution in the South. Weatherford became one of his generation's most effective orators as he visited the major colleges and universities in the South and made the lion and the lamb of science and religion not lie down but rise up together in mutual respect and enlightenment. As International Student Secretary of the YMCA for the colleges of the South and Southwest from 1902 till 1919 and as a leader in student conferences until 1936, he influenced many of the progressive Southerners who became leaders in their region and nation: senators, congressmen, educators, businessmen.

In 1910, when Jim Crow had achieved its tightest stranglehold on the South and the insulation of white consciences from Negro injustices seemed most solid, Weatherford began compiling and publishing some of the first textbooks on Negro life and race relations. Then he began to speak, urging the white South to see what it was doing to itself as well as to the Negro, and he began to work. In 1919 he acted to help found the Commission on Interracial Cooperation, a group of Southern Negroes and whites who worked together for a quarter of a century. Their mutual efforts helped to stamp out lynching, end the cruel farm peonage system, diminish chain gang brutalities, secure better homes and schools and jobs for Negroes, and win more democratic attitudes in whites.

Applying that tough realism which undergirds his idealism, Weatherford came, in 1927, to the Board of Directors of the American Cast Iron Pipe Company in Birmingham, Alabama. Today this company (the largest individual cast-iron pressure-pipe manufacturing plant in the world) is unusual largely because of the success of its attention to human relationships. It has always employed large numbers of Negro workers, and its pioneering plan of profit-sharing has included all of its employees, Negro and white. Weatherford and the company's founder, John J. Eagan, each believed that Christian statesmanship in business pays dividends, in the long run. The financial success of their company proved the soundness of their idealism.

Convinced that education is the strongest single force that can lift people from poverty into plenty, Weatherford built a handsome conference center, Blue Ridge Assembly, in the mountains near Asheville, North Carolina. Here, from 1912 till 1944, when he retired from its presidency, thousands of students and others came under his direct influence in summer conferences and courses of study.

He founded the YMCA Graduate School in Nashville, Tennessee, in 1919, and maintained a high level of academic standards during the seventeen years before it was taken over by neighboring Vanderbilt University. For ten years he was a professor at Fisk University, challenging Negro students to rigid disciplines of study. And for fifty years he has been a member of the Board of Trustees of Kentucky's Berea College. During that time he has brought Berea millions of dollars and—his proudest achievement—hundreds of students he had personally discovered up mountain coves and hillsides, and prodded and inspired to go to college. (The number of times he dug down into his own pocket to help make that decision possible will probably never be recorded anywhere except in the memories of those who received his practical pledge of faith in them.)

Then, while America slept, during its postwar years of international involvements and first tentative thrusts into space, Weatherford woke up again. He looked homeward and found people in deep trouble. Automation, industrialization, the twentieth century had, in some places, caught up with the Appalachia around him and left the people destitute, the countryside desolate.

No one was sure of the extent of Appalachian poverty; indeed, its troubles had not yet been pinpointed and definitively diagnosed. Weatherford proposed to find the facts on the Southern Appalachian region and then act on those findings. He went to the Ford Foundation and in 1957, financed by a $250,000 grant from that foundation, undertook the most comprehensive study ever attempted of all aspects of life in the Southern Appalachian Mountains.

Results of this study were published in 1962 in *The Southern Appalachian Region: A Survey*, written by twenty-two outstanding authorities representing every state in the region. The book promptly became a subject for debate, re-examination, and—of first importance—action. Its impact was important. America had begun to discover its poor—in dark ghettos of the great cities, in land-locked corners of mountain regions, on the neglected fringes of bustling progress and bright prosperity. And here were the facts on one whole segment of the country where too many people had suffered for far too long the eroding and dehumanizing experience of poverty.

In Weatherford's Southern Appalachian survey it was discovered that during the decade from 1940 to 1950 the Southern mountains had lost 1,132,000 people by migration. Not only natural resources had been stripped from the region; its human resources were dwindling, too. And it is these resources that have been Weatherford's concern.

Looking back, we are better able to look forward. Meeting W. D. Weatherford in the framework of history is a challenge, for he refused to submit to the boundaries of "his times." Constantly, consistently, through the better part of a century, he reached beyond the limitations of his moment, the confinements of his generation's habits, mores, fashions, restrictions, into the promise and fulfillment of tomorrow.

And although he has frequently been a prophet, he has never been a saint. His strongest virtues have on occasion become his most vulnerable flaws. The forcefulness of personality which could win converts to a cause and wring money out of impersonal foundations, that same power could also overwhelm less decisive personalities and alienate those of similar drive. If he felt that criticism of his actions was unjustified or unsound, he could cling to his own way as tenaciously as a possum on a persimmon limb—and sometimes as precariously. The point is, he has dared to commit his insight, his foresight, his remarkable capacity for work to an adventure in faith. He has made the greatest gamble of which man is capable: he has staked his talent, his strength, the time of his life on his belief that God is not dead and man is not impotent.

Early in life, consciously or unconsciously, Weatherford seems to have spoken a mighty "Yes" to something beyond his own power. Perhaps the experience was akin to that described by former United Nations Secretary-General Dag Hammarskjold in his autobiographical *Markings*: "I don't know Who—or what—put the question, I don't know when it was put. I don't even remember answering. But at some moment I did answer *Yes* to Someone—or Something—and from that hour I was certain that existence is meaningful and that, therefore, my life, in self-surrender, had a goal."

Whenever, wherever he has been, Weatherford has looked at the people around him and tried to remove blinders of prejudice and provincialism. He has listened and tried to overcome ignorance and indifference. He has grown and tried to take others with him into that creative enterprise.

He is not larger than life, but he is an enlarger of life.

His practicality of method has been equaled by the passion of his purpose. As we move into a decade when our patterns of poverty may become the bleakest want or be resolved into a spacious wisdom of plenty, W. D. Weatherford's life may be a prophecy and a blueprint.

2

East of Dallas, Texas still has a backward glance toward the Old South. Southern memories, customs, and allegiances persist, some strong and obvious, others hidden, fading. West of Fort Worth, however, only thirty miles distant in geography, Texas faces due west. Winds blow off the prairie; yesterday is a bucket of ashes but tomorrow is fire a-kindling.

Weatherford, Texas, sits thirty miles west of Fort Worth, on Rock Creek, which flows into the Brazos River. In 1875 this was still frontier country in many ways. It was hard, good country for a boy to grow up in. There was room to stretch and develop a long reach. There was time to think. There was growth in being carefree and danger in being careless. For those who lived on the wide, lonely acres that spread beyond the town, weather was the first ally or enemy.

On December 1, 1875, winter chill frosted the air. It crept between the great logs of a house on the prairie and settled into corners of the rooms where heat from blazing logs in the deep-throated fireplace reached only fitfully. The house and its people—the mother who lay on her corded bed and wrestled with the forces of life and death, the father, and their five children already

13

born—had braced themselves against weather more bitter than this.

It was a sturdy house, typical of many others dotting the countryside from Virginia and North Carolina to Texas and beyond. Two rooms eighteen feet square were separated by a breezeway twelve feet wide, open at each end. On the Texas frontier this breezeway was also called a dog-trot. The logs of the house had been cut from virgin oak. A steady hand wielding a heavy, sharp-edged adze had squared the logs into heavy timbers. Locust pins held them together. The roof was tight and well made of white oak shingles. At each end of the house stood a wide, tall chimney of stone chinked with clay.

The people who lived here were sturdy, too. They had to be. They were descendants and survivors of men and women who had followed long rocky roads for conscience' sake, who had cleared many a rough acre in their hunger for land, who had never learned to submit humbly to the superiority assumed by any other man. Margaret Jane Turner and Samuel Leonard Weatherford, with their McQueen and Claiborne ancestors, came from a long line of Scotch-Irish pioneers. From North Carolina and Tennessee they had followed the westward trek to Texas. After their marriage they had settled on this small truck farm near Weatherford, named for Samuel's older brother William, and six of their seven children were born here—the next to the last on that raw day in December, 1875: Willis Duke Weatherford.

A paradox of defeat and hope, conflict and cooperation characterized the year and the region into which Weatherford was born. Appomattox was just ten years past. The formal end of Reconstruction was yet two years in the future. Former President Andrew Johnson had recently died, and President U. S. Grant's second term in the White House was drawing to a close. Washington was in turmoil because of rumors of financial fraud and scandal in high places and because of racial clashes that had taken place at the polls and elsewhere throughout the South in recent months.

The Weatherfords might have been poor by today's luxurious standards, but for their time and place they were solid middle-class citizens; at that moment there were many Americans far worse off than they. The panic of 1873 had deepened until thousands of small landowners all across the country were losing their farms. Eight thousand commercial establishments had failed in this year of 1875 alone. An uneasy Congress met in December while white supremacy groups were banding themselves together throughout the South. Rifle Clubs, White Leagues, Knights of the White Camellia, and Ku Klux Klans were springing up in war-ravaged cities, desolate little crossroads villages, and lonely rural enclaves amidst the piney woods or the long bleak stretches of cotton fields. Embittered portions of the white South were organizing in anticipation of the approaching election between Democrat Samuel J. Tilden, Governor of New York, and Republican Rutherford B. Hayes, Governor of Ohio.

Meanwhile, as historian John Hope Franklin has pointed out, "While the white leaders of the South were preoccupied with questions of Negro suffrage and civil rights, Northern financiers and industrialists took advantage of the opportunity to impose their economic control on the South, and it has endured to the present day. The inability of the Negro to solve his problems [during Reconstruction] was not altogether to his discredit. It was merely a symptom of the complexity of the new industrial America which baffled even the most astute of its citizens."

The broadening scope and increasing complexity of

that new industrial America were scarcely yet dreamed of in 1875. There were small inventions whose influence could hardly be foretold.

A young Virginian named James A. Bonsack was devising a machine to manufacture cigarettes—a development that would change the agriculture and industry of a large segment of the South while it altered the social habits of the world. Barbed wire had just been put on the market, and what the cotton gin had been to the development of the South, barbed wire became to the development of the Great Plains. Within the next few years other innovations, large and small, would intensify the industrialization of America and define the character of its culture for future generations. Elevated and subway trains and street cars would speed up concentrations of people into big city complexes; use of refrigerated railway cars would revolutionize the slaughtering, meat-packing, and eating habits of the country; discovery of wireless telegraphy and growing familiarity with the telephone would shrink time and distance. This was a period of bursting physical bonds and expanding material horizons, of sudden riches and the raw scars of a fratricidal war's aftermath.

The South into which Weatherford was born was torn between despair and confidence. It was, above all else, poor. Its per capita wealth was $376 as compared with $1,086 in the states outside the South. Depression was obvious in cities such as New Orleans, where one visitor wrote, "These faces, these faces! One sees them everywhere; on the street, at the theatre, in the salon, in the cars; and pauses for a moment, struck with the expression of entire despair."

On the other hand, there was the confidence that had brought Birmingham, Alabama, into being only four years before, in 1871, "born in an old cornfield of the union of a land company and a railroad." A Philadelphia newspaper gave voice to this optimism, at least for Northern investors going South. In an editorial of 1877 it said: "In the South land, labor, fuel, water power, and building facilities are cheap. The way to clear and large profits is open."

As for Texas, it was simultaneously retrenching and burgeoning. The legacy of war and reconstruction had left it suspicious of legislatures and stingy with schools. Its convention of 1876 rewrote the state constitution and left the legislature in a condition described by one contemporary critic: "The harness is so small, the straps drawn so tight, the check rein pulled to the last buckle hole, and the load to draw so heavy, that the legislative horse will be galled from collar to crupper in the attempt to work, and the State wagon will go creaking along the highway of progress, in the rear of the procession."

Within five years, one Texas newspaper would mourn that there was "scarcely a decent pretense" of a worthy public-school system left in the state, and "the sons and daughters of the poorer classes" were thus condemned to "grow up in ignorance." The railroads and the lumber syndicates were flourishing, however. During these years Texas managed to exhaust virtually all of its vast public domain. It granted to twelve railroad companies alone a tract of more than thirty-two million acres, an area larger than the whole state of Indiana.

The country, the region, the state, all were in the throes of intense turmoil and transition, and many of the problems W. D. Weatherford would devote his life to alleviating had their bitter roots in this dark time of his birth.

Coming of age on a small Texas farm demanded heart and muscle. There were long rows of cotton to hoe and wide acres of corn, watermelons, and sweet potatoes to tend. The corn was raised for feed, but the other crops brought in cash for a year's needs. Each crop might average anywhere from two to five hundred dollars in net returns, depending on the season.

In these fields an unexpected turn of the weather could ruin a year's crop overnight. In winter it could bring a northwester and send the thermometer plummeting thirty or forty degrees in a brief afternoon. A person learned fortitude in accepting nature's blows or blessings.

There was wood to chop and haul and stack for the two big fireplaces, where logs seemed to melt like wax. It was Willis' special duty to keep a supply of wood ahead, and he learned early to hunt out oak and hickory and locust and to by-pass the plentiful sycamore and cottonwood that did not yield a good fire.

There were cows on the farm, for milk; three or four horses, mostly little prairie mustangs; and hogs which were butchered when the weather turned cold in autumn. Brisk mornings whetted a boy's appetite for fresh sausage he had helped grind and hot cakes made from buckwheat he had helped harvest. By the time he was six, the boy was working in his father's fields.

When he was ten years old, Willis asked his father to let him have a plot of land where he could raise watermelons and earn some money of his own. Weatherford, Texas, was proud of its title as watermelon capital of the world, and many a farmer considered the summer a failure if he didn't grow at least one watermelon weighing a hundred pounds or better. His father gave the boy an old garden plot and a big spirited horse, which stood sixteen hands high, to plow it. The season was dry, the land was hard, the horse was strong and willful. The slim boy, wrenched between the unyielding ground and the headstrong horse, did hand-stands on the plow handles, but he got the earth turned. After that, about 4:30 each afternoon when he got home from school, there would be a plow and a horse standing in the field waiting for him. Willis was learning that each new freedom was accompanied by responsibilities.

The boy had his reasons for wanting to make a fast profit in watermelon raising, however. Chief among these hung in the saddle shop downtown: a fine western saddle, with high back and high horn, which he had made up his mind to own some day. Ten cents, fifteen cents at a time he began to save any money that came to his hands. The saddle cost eighteen dollars. On trips to town with his father he would stop by the store and stand for a while looking, refreshing his memory of each detail in its leather and workmanship. Once he asked if he might sit in it for a minute. The storekeeper said no.

Whenever his father went to town, he liked to have Willis go with him to hold the team when they made various stops. The boy took his little cache of money along each time. Not that he considered spending a penny except for that precious saddle, but he liked the feeling of having cash resources at hand when he was in town. One day he went into the largest general store in Weatherford and there his saddle found a rival. He saw a pistol he felt he must have. It cost three dollars and fifty cents. He held the pistol, examined it, then laid it carefully back on the counter and left the store. Down the street he went into that old familiar shop once more and looked at his saddle again. He decided against the pistol.

For almost three years he saved, and when at last Weatherford carried that saddle out of the store it belonged to him in a way that it had never belonged to the shop owner. The impression made on his attitudes and habits by that long process of saving for a single goal was so indelible that he often recounted the experience in later years to influence young people with whom he worked.

The September he was seven years old, Willis entered

the fourth grade of school. Before this he had been tutored at home by his mother, a self-educated woman with only three months of formal schooling. This she had received in a "made-up" subscription school before her family moved from the North Carolina hills.

Willis' first years in school were a disappointment. Staying quiet seemed to be all that was considered necessary for a student's success in the classroom.

In Sunday School each week the situation was even more dreary. His teacher was a fine, dear old soul whose effort at introducing her young charges to the majesty and message of the Bible consisted of handing out miniature picture cards as a reward for perfect attendance or rote memory programs. But there were questions Willis wanted to ask! There were answers he needed to know! He came to resent children's picture cards of Biblical scenes, which were usually insipid and syrupy betrayals rather than portrayals of some of man's greatest religious experiences.

Religion, of course, was no stranger to the Weatherford home. Grandfather John Turner was a hellfire-and-damnation Baptist preacher as well as a Texas farmer. Whenever he came to visit, Willis was allowed to sit up past his usual bedtime and listen to talk of Sam Houston and Davy Crockett, share memories of the North Carolina-Tennessee hills and the chestnuts and chinquapins that grew there in such abundance, reflect on the tarnished condition of man's immortal soul. Turner was a big, fine-looking man, and he made an impression on his grandson.

The summer brush arbor meetings at his other grandmother's also made an impression. Between four and five hundred Methodists gathered almost every summer on the little creek where her farm was located in the country beyond Weatherford. There they enjoyed a uniquely American experience. For a week or more they came together from isolated little farms and the dullness of small-town routine and drudgery to find fellowship with each other and have their religious spirit revived. The women slept in the family wagons; the men and boys slept on the ground below. Preaching was in progress all day long every day and far into the evenings, with four, five, six sermons each day.

At one lively meeting an elderly woman who "got religion" became so excited she reached up and pulled a wilting tree limb out of the roof that provided rough shelter from the sun and rain. Brush in hand, she marched up and down the aisle beating people on back and shoulders. "Do you feel it?" she shouted. "Do you feel it?" The boy was embarrassed by her display, but he certainly did like her spirit. Enthusiasm was something he could always share.

During the summer he was eight, Willis Weatherford walked forward at the close of a sermon and affirmed that he wanted to join the church. He had given no one any prior inkling of his intentions. His mother, sitting across the aisle, and the rest of his family were completely surprised by his move. But it was not unusual for very young children to make this momentous religious decision when there was an able, appealing preacher in the pulpit, as there was on this occasion.

Weatherford, however, unlike many of his contemporaries who made such youthful commitments under the emotional influence of a sultry summer evening, sweet music, and soaring oratory, somehow avoided the conviction that he had now "found God" once and for all and could presently proceed, to all practical intent and purpose, to forget Him. Rather, the boy had only taken on faith the first formal step toward a long passage of discovery that would lead the man into an ever-enlarging knowledge of his Creator and his fellow man.

In the autumn of 1888, the boy's father traded their

farm for a store and a stock of merchandise, and the family moved into town. Instead of the old log home they had known they now lived in a frame house with a small yard where chinaberry and maple trees grew. Instead of fireplaces they now had stoves. Their fuel, however, was still wood, and it was still Willis' chore to provide it. His mother had inherited a few acres of woodland out in the country, and so from time to time he went there to cut and haul supplies of wood. Sometimes in summer as he worked to lay in a winter's supply he took a wagon and team and went to the country for several days alone. He cooked his meals on an open fire. He enjoyed the solitude of long starry nights and strenuous days. And whenever he paused to rest from cutting and working up the trees, he read. Books were becoming an essential part of his daily life.

When he was twelve years old he entered the seventh grade and met Henry Brevard. The moment Weatherford stepped into his room he knew that this teacher cared about him, about what happened to him. Brevard taught people, not books. He was a tall, slim man with an alert, expressive face, a graduate of Bowling Green State College in Kentucky. And he was young. He brought the classroom alive for Willis and his other pupils and provided a lifelong example of the inspiration education may be for a young person who falls under the right teacher's influence.

The year after he finished Henry Brevard's class Willis worked as cashier in his father's store. Since the town was a market for cotton and many farmers bought their farm and household supplies for a whole year as soon as they had sold their cotton, some of the bills Willis had to make out were impressively large for a boy's inexperienced handling. After the first few trials, when neither his exacting Scotch father nor his older brother Robert, who was a partner in the store, found it necessary to correct any work he did, Willis gained confidence. He was playing a man's role in a man's world. No one thought to commend or encourage him in this new job. In the Weatherford household it went without saying that a man did not undertake work he couldn't do—and do right. Willis learned to achieve without expectation of applause. He also learned to listen to the opinions and reminiscences of the older men as they came and went in the store.

While he worked as cashier, Willis made up his mind that he was going to college. He had entertained vague plans about college for a long time, but they were suddenly crystallized by an incident that took place in the store one afternoon.

Willis and his father were working together when one of the leading citizens of the town came in and asked for a donation to local Weatherford College. Short on cash at the moment, Willis' father had to refuse the request. Stung by the independent Scotsman's blunt reply, the visitor said, "You should be more interested than I am in supporting this college. My son isn't even going to Weatherford. He's going to Vanderbilt University. But I imagine your boy will have to go to college here if he goes anywhere—and I should think you'd want to see that it stays open."

The man's condescension and arrogance infuriated Willis. If that man had known the Weatherfords better, he would have realized that nothing could insure this boy's graduation from Vanderbilt as surely as the haughty assumption that he *couldn't* go there. Willis made plans for his educational future.

Weatherford College was a small institution roughly equivalent to a present-day high school and junior college combined. It awarded the B.S. and B.A. degrees. Willis lived at home and went to school there for five years.

The year he entered the college as a pupil, another young Texan came as a teacher. His name was John A. Lomax; he had had one year of previous college training (his only entire year in any school), and he would go on to the University of Texas and become internationally famous as a collector and singer of American ballads. For six years Lomax worked in the "preparatory department" of Weatherford College, and he has left us a brief but vivid vignette of the atmosphere he found. The description might have fit many of the small private and church educational institutions scattered through the South and Southwest at that time.

"Professor Switzer," Lomax said, "and his faculty of seven persons struggled to instruct two hundred to four hundred students from their a-b-c's until they 'finished' fifteen years later. Again no library, no laboratories worthy of the name, more teachers with meager training."

Lomax left one clear memory with Willis Weatherford. After an examination in physiology he returned the papers to class and explained, "Only one student made a 100 on this test. Because I don't believe any paper can be perfect, however, I gave him only 99." When Willis was handed his examination with the 99 on it, he was sharply disappointed. Memory of that experience did not restrain him, years later, from grading just as strictly, however.

Facilities at the little college were limited, strict rules were rigidly enforced, the faculty was overworked, but Lomax later recalled "those eager boys and girls" of the student body. His recollections were tinged with both pride and shame: pride in their eagerness and shame at what he felt to be his incompetence as a teacher at that time. Apparently there was something stirring in those students (several of whom went on to achieve political and educational careers of distinction), something recent jargon would describe as "motivation." It overrode lack of laboratories or faculty Ph.D. degrees.

His family and friends had realized that Willis was an unusually ambitious boy who was also interested in ideas. He could play pranks with the best of the boys, frighten his mother into speechlessness by leaping off the highest barn roof on the farm during a game of follow-the-leader, and go on hunts with men and boys in the neighborhood. But it was the serious side of his nature that was dominant. There was a tacit agreement among the family that Willis would enter the ministry. This was the accepted calling for any young man who had a philosophical turn of mind, interest in the condition of his fellow creatures—and meager cash resources.

Willis had no particular objection to becoming a Methodist minister, but there was one thing in which he did have a most particular interest and that was securing the best education he could take. This resolve brought him into direct conflict with his father.

When Weatherford had completed his sophomore year at Weatherford College, the professor who was his adviser told him that he should take up the study of Greek. Willis knew that this was a fundamental subject, and he had a passion for fundamentals. He longed to take Greek.

At home he told his family of the professor's advice. A family council was called, as it frequently was when there were momentous decisions to be made. His father, older brother Robert who had had three years of college, older sister Virginia who had graduated from Peabody College in Nashville, and the oldest sister Flora, as well as his mother, gathered on the front porch to discuss whether Willis should undertake the study of Greek, with all the expense, time, and energy this would involve.

His father stated at once that he saw no reason why

the boy should study Greek. It would be foolish when there was no hope that he would go on through any college beyond the one there in town, certainly not through graduate study or work at any theological seminary. In addition, the older man went on, Matthew Neely had preached what everyone said was the greatest sermon ever delivered on the floor of the Methodist General Conference, and he had had no more education then than Willis had already had.

There was silence for a moment after their father had spoken, and then Willis said, "But think what Matthew Neely could have done if he had been really educated!"

One by one his brother and sisters agreed, however, that it would be foolish, indeed presumptuous, for him to study this ancient language. Their discussion lasted an hour or longer. Through it all his mother sat quietly by, thin, erect, her hair smoothed back tightly from her lined but gentle face. Her keen blue eyes looked at each of her family and at her intense and eager next-to-youngest child. She understood that this decision involved more than the study of Greek. It might influence the drive energizing Willis' future commitment. It could reveal the depth or shallowness of his self-confidence.

The family conference ended with the general assumption that it would be useless for Willis to study Greek.

As the others left the porch and Willis followed them, his mother nudged his elbow. He looked around and met her direct gaze. She spoke for the first time. "If you want to take Greek, you take it!"

And he took it.

His mother had shown him that poverty of opportunity was of less consequence than poverty of determination.

3

As Weatherford grew up he had the benefit of two environments that have been basic to the American experience, although each seems to be fast approaching extinction now. He knew rural farm life in the deep country, and he knew life in a small town.

Growing up on a farm with daily dependence on weather and land and crops, he learned how fragile man's hopes and plans may be in the larger scheme of nature—and he also learned how tough a man must be simply to survive in the contest with nature. He knew the loneliness of woods and plains and the horizons a book can open to a searching mind.

When Weatherford's family moved from the country and he shifted work from his father's fields to his general store, and then when he attended the local college, he discovered that a small thriving community deep in the provinces near the turn of the century provided a cross section of human nature in depth and variety. He watched, listened, questioned.

There were those of whom their fellow townsfolk spoke with special respect and awe, such as the newly made millionaire who still went to his bank in his shirt sleeves and rode through town with fifteen or twenty yelping fox-hounds following after his horse.

Once when Weatherford needed a small loan from the bank to continue his work at the college, he asked his brother Robert if it would be all right to go to this important man with his problem. "Go ahead," Robert replied. "As long as you're honest and hard-working, no man is too big to talk to you about anything that interests you." Willis went and got his loan and often remembered his older brother's advice during later years when he was going to talk to influential men about problems that "interested" him.

There was the intellectual elite of the town: a lawyer who later became Chief Justice of the Texas Supreme Court, and the lawyer's brother-in-law, S. W. T. Lanham, who was a United States congressman for many years. When Weatherford's father took him to visit the congressman one day, the latter gave the young man advice that proved more valuable than any tangible memento he could have bestowed. "Make yourself a good speaker, boy," he said. "No one can be a success as a public man unless he can express his ideas with force!"

Weatherford had already joined the literary society in his school, but now he redoubled his efforts and resolved to speak at every opportunity. On one occasion he and the congressman's son, who were classmates, made up the team that went to a nearby city for intercollegiate debate. They lost, because of his own rather than his partner's shortcomings Weatherford felt, and after that he worked even harder and practiced even longer. One night when a man who lived near the college spied a dim light burning in the auditorium of the otherwise darkened building and hurried to investigate, he peeped in the window and saw Weatherford standing on the platform addressing a room full of empty seats. His ringing words were accompanied by the most energetic gestures. The spectator left without interrupting the young speaker's practice. Those long nights of work would eventually pay off for Weatherford as he stood on platforms around the world and spoke to seats that were not empty.

And what good was a small town that didn't have its public iconoclasts and "characters?" The two in his town who made sharp impressions on Weatherford were the self-proclaimed atheists. One, a lawyer, was acknowledged to be the best speaker in town while the other held the distinction of being the only man who wore a silk stove-pipe hat. At that time religious unorthodoxy could turn into a full-time career—and outright social ostracism. Even then, however, Weatherford believed that no person was ever better understood by isolation.

"Those holding different religious views at that time needed full and thorough communication," he has said, "no less than those holding unpopular political and social views need to communicate today. Problems are not solved by isolation but by long, hard, conscientious work toward resolution."

The year they were juniors in school Weatherford and three of his favorite classmates—John Marshall, one of the school leaders; pretty Daisy Smith, who was daughter of the town cotton buyer; and Annie Yeager, a quiet, delicate girl—sat together at the spring commencement exercises. That night both Annie Yeager and W. D. Weatherford won the coveted senior awards, given each year to the boy and girl of the junior class who had made the best all-around record. Because this honor carried not only prestige but also cash to meet all tuition and expenses for the senior year, it was doubly welcomed by Weatherford, who had been hard-pressed each term to earn his tuition as well as his top grades and carry his share of the work-load at home. Practical as well as idealistic, Weatherford liked to recall this incident during later years in dealing with young people. Honors might be icing on the cake for delight, but cash was bread and meat for survival in the race.

One evening when Governor Robert Taylor of Tennessee spoke on the local Chautauqua program, Annie Yeager's uncle, Ben Akard, who had been born in the mountains of East Tennessee and was a boyhood neighbor of Taylor's, entertained him. Bob Taylor was one of the most popular public speakers of his time. He, a Democrat, and his brother Alfred, a Republican, had run against each other for office of Governor of Tennessee. Their race in 1886 had made folk history with its wit and oratory. From this experience Bob had composed a nationally known lecture, "The Fiddle and the Bow," which he delivered in many parts of the country. Weatherford was to take Annie Yeager to hear this program, and when he went to call for Ben Akard's niece, Mr. Akard introduced him to the famous orator and politician. The governor with the white mustache and patriarchal manner looked at Weatherford a moment and then turned to his host. "Ben," he said, "when I was a boy I loved your wife just like this young fellow loves your niece!"

Embarrassment flushed Weatherford's cheeks, but if he had to be teased it was certainly pleasant to be the scapegoat of such a famous and jovial man. And that night, at the lecture, Weatherford received another lesson in the power of the spoken word, the importance of the platform as a classroom, a stage, and a battleground all rolled into one.

If Weatherford did feel romantic affection for Annie, his feelings had no time to ripen. At the end of their senior year the young girl died of tuberculosis. Her early death was in many ways a symbolic foreshadowing of the tragic events that would subsequently overtake the two great loves he would know in his maturity.

At his graduation from Weatherford College he was class valedictorian. Now he was ready to go on to Vanderbilt and more education.

More education called for more money. He had already accumulated a backlog of debts for the school work just completed. He decided to repay these before looking to Vanderbilt. Plans could be postponed as long as it was perfectly clear that they were not being abandoned. He stood examination for a state teacher's certificate and headed into the Texas back country for three years of teaching wherever he could find a job.

The first year, from September, 1894, till spring, 1895, he was principal of a two-teacher elementary school some thirty miles from Weatherford. Many of his students, who carried in drinking water in a bucket and piled up wood for the stove during the winter, were older than he was. He grew side whiskers which helped make him appear older than his years. When he was confronted with his first case of cheating, compounded by lying, he administered a sound thrashing to the almost-grown boy involved, and that settled his discipline problems.

The following school term from September to March, Weatherford was on the prairie northeast of his home town in a small farm community. The one-room school where he taught accommodated some fifty pupils of all ages. Its influence ranged far beyond its limited student body and formal classes, however. The school and the church were the vital social and cultural centers of each settlement at this time. If they did not bring opportunities to the starved little villages and communities scattered across the country, adults and children alike went without.

In his school Weatherford organized community meetings. Eagerly the people came, filling the hard benches and listening with rapt attention to the recitations, talks, or other little programs the young teacher had arranged. They responded with special enthusiasm to debates on local and national issues. Weatherford began to glimpse the hunger for self-improvement that stirred in those who were given a chance to satisfy it.

During his two terms in this community he boarded in farm homes where he read by oil lamp late into the winter nights. He studied book after book of history and literature, working toward his entrance into Vanderbilt University.

Then, in the spring of 1897, he was stricken with typhoid fever. And his eyes failed him.

Apparently he had picked up the typhoid germ during his last days of teaching in the country, for after only a few days at home he fell ill. No sickness was more dreaded at that time than typhoid. If it did not result in immediate death, recuperation was painfully slow and often left some lifelong disability in its wake. Perhaps there is no better concrete demonstration of the changes Weatherford's life has embraced than this example of the illness which almost destroyed him in young manhood. Typhoid, then the plague of so much of America, is so nearly blotted out today that most people do not even know its symptoms.

During long days and nights of fever and delirium, his sisters, a neighbor woman, and his mother undertook the task of nursing him.

Once he heard the woman who was a neighbor ask the deliberate, white-haired doctor, "How is he?"

"I'm afraid he'll be dead within the hour."

But all during that critical night his mother bathed his face with cold water, never allowing him to lapse into sleep and succumb to the fever which was breaking. The doctor's prediction, like the unfounded rumor of Mark Twain's death, was greatly exaggerated. Perhaps it had failed to take into account Willis Weatherford's tough physique or the devotion of Willis' mother.

These two came through the bleak disappointment concerning Willis' eyesight, too. When the doctor told Weatherford that he must rest his eyes from April until September, the young man was stunned. He protested that during the summer months he must read a full course in history and economics and literature, for he hoped to achieve advanced standing when he enrolled at Vanderbilt in the fall. The doctor said that this was out of the question. Then Margaret Jane Turner Weatherford quietly reassured her son. "All that you'd meant to read for yourself this summer, I'll read aloud to you."

She did just that. Hundreds of pages of subjects she had never encountered before, scores of books of which she had never heard, she read to him. And when he entered Vanderbilt University in September, he was placed in the junior class.

4

When Willis D. Weatherford arrived in Nashville, Tennessee, in 1897, the fifty dollars in cash which was his chief tangible asset was not as minute a sum as it might seem today. Every aspect of education in the South at that moment—and for years to come—was plagued by poverty of funds and abundance of need.

There were, for instance, in proportion to the adult population, twice as many children to educate in the South as in the North. Taxable wealth, on the other hand, was so much less in the South that its school rates would have to be five times as large as those in the North to provide equal school funds. There were more than three and a half million illiterates in the South: approximately 12 per cent of its white population and nearly 50 per cent of its Negro population. As for the higher institutions of learning, some measure of their plight is suggested by the fact that the total annual income of sixty-six colleges and universities in seven Southern states was less than the income enjoyed by Harvard University alone. Not one of the nation's eighteen colleges or universities with endowments of $1½ million or more was in the South. Only two of the thirty that had $1 million endowments were Southern. One of these was Tulane, in New Orleans—and the other was Vanderbilt.

Average annual salary for professors in forty-four of the better Southern colleges was approximately $840. It was perhaps something of a miracle that the Southern institutions could achieve any educational victories at all, but win they did, and one reason doubtless was to be found in the character of many of the professors. As one historian has pointed out, "What the clergymen and gentlemen on teaching staffs lacked in technical training and scholarship was compensated for by their striking personalities, genteel worldliness, and high ethics. Such characteristics probably were more impressive to many students than a greater amount of scholarship."

It was such men that Weatherford would encounter at Vanderbilt, along with many, of course, whose scholarly attainments ranked high above the regional average. At this time there were five members of the faculty who had studied in Leipzig and received the rigorous German discipline. Few Southern institutions could boast of similar riches.

Nashville itself, in the autumn of 1897, was in the midst of celebrating Tennessee's centennial. President McKinley had visited the city in May and opened the exposition observing the first century of statehood: 1796–1896. During the six months that the Centennial Park was open, more than six million people came to see the exhibits in a complex of buildings grouped around a plaster reproduction of the Greek Parthenon. This Parthenon would remain in existence as a symbol of Nashville's claim to be "the Athens of the South." One reason for this claim lay in the number of educational institutions in the city. Two of its most widely respected, Vanderbilt and Fisk, a Negro university, would play a very specific role in Weatherford's life. In fact, the entire spectrum of higher education in the South would become a matter of personal knowledge and concern to

35

Weatherford as he spent the next twenty years visiting campuses throughout the region.

Vanderbilt, in 1897, was observing its twenty-fifth anniversary. Three years before Weatherford was born, the Methodist Episcopal Church South had chartered it as Central University; but when, the following year, Bishop Holland N. McTyeire prevailed upon Cornelius Vanderbilt to endow the school with $500,000, and this sum was later increased to one million, the university's name had been changed to honor its benefactor.

The two most important men, then, in this first quarter of a century of the university's life had been the famous New York tycoon, Cornelius Vanderbilt, who furnished it a financial foundation, and a chancellor named James H. Kirkland, who provided it with strict intellectual and spiritual fundamentals and stern scholarly standards. With admission qualifications at a new low in many Southern colleges, Chancellor Kirkland insisted on adequate preparation for entrance to Vanderbilt. In 1895 he had taken the lead in organizing the Southern Association of Colleges and Secondary Schools, which was "to elevate the standard of scholarship and to effect uniformity of entrance requirements." Kirkland obviously did not wish to go along with the first half of an apt observation made by one of his fellow college presidents about this time: "We are liberal about letting young men into the freshman class but particular about letting them out."

The chancellor was one of the outstanding educators of the South and the nation during the first decades of this century. F. C. Rand, Chairman of the Board of Trustees of Vanderbilt, summed up Kirkland's contribution and something of his character, in these words: "The period of his chancellorship was not an easy one. From beginning to the end it was filled with obstacles to be overcome. The controversy with the church; the preservation of the integrity of the University as a school of scholarly attainments; the search for needed funds; the struggle to maintain and elevate the standard of education in the South and in the nation—in a word—the struggle to meet the exacting demands of the inspired soul within him made him say when he laid the burden down: 'I leave to my successor the task of completing old undertakings and of initiating new ones. If I may take an illustration from my own garden which I love so well, I leave to my successor no bed of roses, but a hoe and a plow, and an uncultivated field.'"

After his first introduction to both Vanderbilt and its chancellor, Weatherford was glad that he had made, with his mother's help, that intensive effort of preparation for entrance to the university. And it was in his nature to expect that the school would be "particular about letting him out."

Shy, awkward, conscientious country boys from staunch Methodist families throughout the South were plentiful at Vanderbilt during that period, especially in the School of Religion. Most of them were as proud as they were provincial, ambitious, responsible, accustomed to hard work—and none more so than the young man who arrived from middle Texas one mellow day in September, walked down the shaded paths and adjusted himself to this big campus, this capital city so different from the small town and familiar school and wide-rolling spaces he had previously known. He was tall and slim, muscular from work outdoors, with brown hair parted in the middle above a high forehead and wide blue eyes. His family expected Willis to major in religious studies. He himself expected to work toward a degree in philosophy. As it turned out, his major study was literature.

During his first year at Vanderbilt, Weatherford lived in the five-story building of the Department of Theology, Wesley Hall. He paid for his room by tending the gas system for the building, lighting it and putting it out each night. His board cost him ten dollars a month.

Weatherford, who always enjoyed good food, found the fare drab, but he was in no position to complain. He could, however, relish the brief grace a young theological student offered one night at supper when, in a moment of mischief that almost brought on his expulsion, he said, "Lord, we thank Thee for what we wish we were about to receive. Amen."

His second, and senior, year Weatherford was made an assistant instructor in the gymnasium under physical education professor Dr. J. T. Gwathmey. A private home near the university provided him room and board for some twenty-five dollars a month, part of which he could pay with his instructor's salary. The rest he had to borrow.

Under Dr. William M. Baskerville, who had been a member of the original Vanderbilt faculty, Weatherford read Shakespeare and began an intensive study of Southern literature. He wrestled with Greek and mathematics, received his Phi Beta Kappa key, and after winning his B.A. degree promptly set to work on graduate study. Although Dean Wilbur F. Tillett of the Vanderbilt School of Religion assumed he would matriculate there, Weatherford had decided that a doctorate in philosophy would provide a much broader education than he could get in a theological college. He felt that if he went on to work with other people a Ph.D. degree could secure him a wide and attentive audience. In addition there was his hunger for literature, philosophy, sociology, and comparative religion.

He went to talk over plans for his work toward advanced degrees with Dr. James H. Kirkland, who could be cold as a wedge of steel but also just and wise. The chancellor rubbed his head thoughtfully, then told

Weatherford: "Well, we can't give you all the advantages of Harvard for graduate study, but we can work you just as hard!"

Weatherford had learned the discipline of hard work on that Texas farm and in the lonely little rural schools where he had taught. Now it stood him in good stead as he plunged into a rigorous schedule of classes, research, athletics, and work to earn his way through graduate school.

Dante, Browning, Carlyle, Ruskin, and Tennyson became intimate acquaintances. Weatherford's master's thesis was a comparison of Hawthorne the Puritan with George Eliot the Positivist. His doctoral dissertation, later published as a book, analyzed the philosophical principles in Browning. Robert Browning's poetic voice of faith and optimism might have been Weatherford's own, so congenial were their thoughts and beliefs. Browning's affirmations exerted a strong influence on the young student's life.

But Weatherford did not spend all his time communing with Browning or conferring with the erudite German-trained Dr. Richard Jones, who was his English department mentor and the most challenging professor Weatherford encountered at Vanderbilt. Under the spell of the famous YMCA Secretary Fletcher Brockman, Weatherford had joined that organization while he was at Weatherford College. At Vanderbilt he became the first graduate student to be elected president of the YMCA. He held the office for two years. His popularity with fellow students was also demonstrated when he was chosen to be president of the Graduate Club, and for three years he was worthy master of his fraternity.

He was also earning his living and participating in the expanding athletic program of the university. The first day he returned to Vanderbilt to begin his graduate work, Dr. Gwathmey, his old gymnasium instructor, came to see him. Explaining that he was resigning to take a much better paying job in New York, Gwathmey asked Weatherford to go with him to see Chancellor Kirkland, for he wanted to suggest that his young assistant be appointed to take his place. The chancellor agreed to this proposition, and with two assistants Weatherford served as head of the gymnasium during his three years of graduate study. All the men at the university, including football and baseball players, had to take these courses. During this time, Weatherford also coached the first basketball team at Vanderbilt.

At the end of two undergraduate and three graduate years, Weatherford had won his three degrees at Vanderbilt and had accumulated a debt of $1,908. He had also met a beautiful girl named Lula Belle Trawick. Her father was a physician in Nashville, and she was a college graduate of quiet charm and grace.

Weatherford had also, during this time, made his first friendships with Negroes. Much of the manual labor around the university was done by Negroes, but Weatherford was no stranger to manual labor himself and this raised no barrier between him and some of the men he often stopped to talk with. Robert Wingfield, head cook at West Side Row (a series of cottages each housing sixteen students) where Weatherford lived for a time, became his friend. Each year just before Christmas holidays Wingfield gave a Christmas dinner for a few chosen students. He bought the food and prepared it himself, and the half-dozen or so men honored by Wingfield's invitation considered it one of the great occasions of campus life. During Weatherford's first year as a graduate student he was invited to this Christmas dinner. From that moment on he became a friend and confidant of many of the Negro employees of Vanderbilt. With growing awareness he began to see a minority people whose problems the rest of the South would evade at its own peril, whose potential the South would stifle to its own impoverishment. And he did not see them in grand impersonal abstractions but in terms of warm human relationships.

In March, 1902, just before taking his Ph.D. degree, Weatherford received a telegram from Dr. John R. Mott, head of the international YMCA. He was surprised and flattered that Mott, one of the leading Christian statesmen of his day, should even know he existed. The telegram asked Weatherford not to accept any other offer of employment until Mott's assistant, Hans Anderson, could come south and talk with him.

In April, Anderson arrived in Nashville. He had a long visit with Weatherford, then offered him the job of International YMCA Student Secretary for the colleges of the South and Southwest. This included work in some two hundred colleges in fourteen states. Mott, through Anderson, asked Weatherford to accept for a ten-year term. The younger man would agree to only three years. "We'll see what the future holds," he said.

So Willis Weatherford, recently a student, was to become a molder of students. He dreamed of making the word "religion" meaningful in a way that it had not been before to thousands of young people. But he could not do this *en masse*. He knew he would have to establish personal contact with those on whom he wished to make any lasting impression.

During his years at Vanderbilt he himself had undergone at least one long dry season of tortuous doubt, and he had found no one to whom he could turn for reasoned discussion and help during this crisis. Now he hoped to provide that help to some other young person who might be struggling through a similar ordeal.

It was his own Browning who had said, "A man's reach should exceed his grasp, or what's a heaven for?" And after all, until a man had reached out and out and out, how could he be sure what his limitations, or his capabilities, really were?

5

"No amount of interest in matters that are occurring in this world can be an effective substitute for an intelligent concern in matters that lie within the sphere of the world to come." This pronouncement by an editor of one of the denominational publications in the South expressed the general attitude of the church at this time in its clear-sighted focus on eternity and its myopia with regard to the present.

C. Vann Woodward, perceptive historian of the South, has described the atmosphere as it existed at the turn of the century and for several decades to follow: "Neither learning nor literature of the secular sort could compare with religion in power and influence over the mind and spirit of the South. The exuberant religiosity of the Southern people, the conservative orthodoxy of the dominant sects, and the overwhelming Protestantism of all but a few parts of the region were forces that persisted powerfully in the twentieth century."

These forces clashed with equally powerful forces that were abroad in the land, especially the Darwinian theory of evolution and the higher criticism, as it came to be called, which applied new and strict intellectual standards to fresh discoveries and interpretations of

42

ancient history. The dilemma of the doctrinal dispute over evolution has been summed up thus by Francis Butler Simkins: "To Southern conservatives Darwinism seemed to usurp a sacred prerogative of religion by attempting to explain origins and destinies, and by lowering man to the level of animals without the personal moral responsibility of Christianity. To Southern liberals, on the other hand, Darwinism seemed to offer the church an opportunity to discharge its historic mission of reconciling dogma with accepted scientific doctrine."

Colleges and universities of the South were in this period of fundamental struggle when Weatherford began his journeys to the campuses of the region. Some professors had already lost their positions for maintaining that "the Bible does not teach science and that a sympathetic understanding of the theory of evolution does not lead to doubt but to a more profound reverence for God's plan of creation," or for filing a minority dissent to the prevailing political and racial proscriptions. Students were caught up in a ferment of change and growth. Yet change of any sort was precisely what many people feared and resented most.

Weatherford was peculiarly well equipped to work with young people at this time. His energy was more than equal to their vigorous demands. The keenest among them were troubled, questioning, dissatisified with repetition of old dogmas which denied new facts and which were often blind to the realities around them. Weatherford's religious convictions were emotionally and intellectually rooted in the soundest traditions of the past, but they also reached out to embrace the expanding possibilities of the future. In his fiery talks to questing or lethargic students he flung out new challenges for man to increase in knowledge of himself and the universe and to grow in social concern for each other.

The campuses he visited were often poor, starved of

sufficient funds, faculty, or equipment; but as Weatherford stood on their platforms year after year and looked into the faces of their young people, he knew they held the region's most valuable resource, its youth, its next generation. They were the force which would bring about change.

More than half a century later, the dean emeritus of one of the largest state universities recalled something of the atmosphere which prevailed during the first decade of the century, when Weatherford visited the college where this man was a professor.

"College curricula continued," he said, "to give main importance to the languages and mathematics, but the physical sciences were receiving more and more attention. At the small college I had attended, a 'Science Hall' was added to the campus, and a young professor of Physics and Chemistry was added to the faculty. What had been true for some years, no doubt, became more noticeable, namely that the facts of science disputed Biblical representations in the realm of nature. But, as I recall, the disturbing contradictions were not taken so seriously. It has been an interesting fact that I have observed in this connection: a good many fairly intelligent college graduates developed what I have termed the bicameral mind, so they could talk in Biblical language or in the terms of science.

"Following, or to some degree coinciding with adjustment to the light of new views in the realm of nature, we found ourselves facing problems presented by the results of historical criticism that applied to the whole ancient world. Here the bicameral mind furnished no help. A new and enlightening intelligence came to many from their understanding and accepting the light afforded by the higher criticism. But for many then, and still in this day, the results of the scholars' study seemed destructive of Christians' faith in the Bible.

44

"It was at this time that Dr. Weatherford gave distinguished service through his lectures, and perhaps more by his personal conferences, in clearing the minds of inquiring students from harassing doubts by redeeming intelligence."

Up and down and across fourteen Southern states Weatherford journeyed, from Virginia to Oklahoma and Texas, from Kentucky to Louisiana and Florida, visiting every major college and all the state universities, a total of some seventy-five each year.

At the larger schools he tried to stay at least three or four days on each visit. He made two, three, sometimes four talks a day. At first these were given mainly to the YMCA groups, but by the beginning of his second year of travel Weatherford had been invited by the president of every college he had visited up to that time to speak to the entire student body.

"He covered the South like a Paul Revere," one student recalled later, "only W. D. Weatherford went too fast to be bothered with the horse."

Assembly periods normally lasted for three-quarters of an hour. Weatherford packed all the vigor and conviction he could muster into those forty-five minutes. He read a short passage from a flexible New Testament that he carried in his pocket. Then, laying the book on the speaker's stand, he would launch into his subject, and without notes or repetition or hesitation he held his audience as he shared with them a vision of what their lives might become. He used personal experiences and anecdotes to keep his talk practical.

In the beginning it was not always easy to get the initial attention of administration or students. Weatherford felt that many students showed little interest in religion because they had been exposed only to its emotional appeals. They had grown deaf to the jargon many religious leaders imposed upon them. Weatherford resolved to find ways to make young people listen. The method he used at one college was typical of other encounters.

The president of the college was one of the leaders of his church denomination, narrow in his theology and limited in his capacity for courtesy. He had invited Weatherford to speak at the chapel hour, but then he informed the men who were arranging the schedule that there was no need to call an evening meeting, for he was sure no students would attend.

When Weatherford heard about this, his Scotch-Irish anger blazed. He sought out one of the students he knew, a boy who was earning his school tuition and board by running a pressing club, and told him that he thought his college president had greatly underestimated the students. Could this boy find a gym suit Weatherford might borrow for a little while?

Now Weatherford was fresh out of Vanderbilt's athletic department, where he had served as instructor for three years. He was hard and muscular. That afternoon he went down to the college gymnasium. When he found the coach, Weatherford asked him to get together a few of his best athletes. Then Weatherford challenged these prime fellows to a work-out. Before the giant swings, the bar vaults, the push-ups, and the other exercises were half finished, most of the student body had gathered to watch or to participate.

After supper it was announced in every dormitory that Weatherford would speak that night. The auditorium was filled. Students and faculty discovered that if Weatherford could give them a strenuous work-out on the gym floor, he could give them no less an energetic work-out from the platform. He spoke to their daily experiences in a language that lifted their ambitions. Whenever he returned to that campus in subsequent years, he found a ready audience.

Just as influential as his public speeches were his personal interviews. During the afternoon, following a morning's talks, and far into the night after an evening lecture, Weatherford would meet with anyone who sought his attention.

Problems the students brought him ranged from the trivial to the tragic. They were intimate and intense. One of the most despairing students who ever came to him had wrecked a professor's marriage. Another had committed unpremeditated murder and gone unpunished except in the labyrinths of his own conscience. Sometimes they prefaced their conversations by stating that they had not come to talk about religion, but as they went on to pour out their troubles and dilemmas, Weatherford understood that their concept of religion was too small if they believed it was not involved in these experiences.

Weatherford realized the need for leaders in the South. Wherever he went he sought out those young people who had shown qualities of leadership. He pointed out to them that the greatest yearning in man's life is for spiritual values and commitment. He assured them that this could not be achieved by man's smallest efforts. "To be satisfied," he often said, "is the prelude to being dead. Hell is not a burning flame, but complete lack of love, lack of aspiration, lack of motive to do better." They could create their own hell right here on earth.

At several of the colleges where Weatherford spoke, cheating had become a major problem. It was so prevalent that discovery had taken on the aspect of a game between faculty and students with each vying to see which could devise the most ingenious methods for outwitting the other. As he became aware of this situation, Weatherford added a lecture to his schedule and new thoughts to his personal conferences.

He dared students to realize that character is as contagious as smallpox. He appealed to common sense (the cheater becomes himself the cheated if he "gets by" on anything less than his own knowledge) and asserted one of his basic convictions: "No man who is a real Christian tries to just get by. Whether a person is a student, a businessman, a minister, or a housewife, to just 'get by' is to be a real sinner. Until each person takes seriously his program of work, we will continue to have a slap-dash world which neither pleases God nor serves man." Professors and young people told him that cheating on the campuses he visited declined markedly.

College administrators and faculty were frequently under pressure from ecclesiastical and political influences who wanted knowledge dispensed only in accordance with certain established rules and approved patterns. Weatherford brought these harassed men fresh stimulus to live up to their own intellectual standards.

On one occasion Weatherford was met at the train by the president of the university, who had asked to entertain this visitor in his home. Each night, after a full day's schedule, the two men sat down together and talked. The president had received his Ph.D. degree from Yale University and was considered one of the South's outstanding scholars and administrators, yet the new historical criticism and psychology of religion studies that seemed to question many of the traditional religious beliefs had raised doubts in this man's mind about his own convictions. (His father-in-law, unafflicted by questions *or* tolerance, a powerful bishop of the church, had settled quickly on a method for handling such disruptive tendencies. "He says," the young administrator confided in Weatherford ruefully, "that I'm a 'damned heretic. Let's burn him!' ") Weatherford had already resolved these dilemmas in his own mind and understood the compatibility, indeed necessity, of searching out both scientific and religious truth. By listening sympathetically and recounting his own experiences he was able to bring the educator a new insight into humanity's evolving awareness of God.

It is difficult today to understand the curtain of intellectual caution and conformity which surrounded many Southern institutions a half-century ago and to appreciate the cataclysms which accompanied change. One eminent philosophy professor of the time said, "When I learned that Jesus was probably not a Methodist, it was a jar."

Weatherford felt that religion should be made relevant to the questions of the times. He had no patience with a doctrine or faith that tranquilized where it should transform, anesthetized where it should electrify.

To his youthful audiences he said, "Too many people spend Sunday morning praying on their knees and the rest of the week preying on their neighbors." And he expanded the term "neighbor" to include all other human beings.

One student, B. E. Mitchell, who later went on to become a well-known professor of mathematics at the University of Mississippi, remembers, "Dr. Weatherford's word to us was: 'Look!' And with that he showed us new horizons of achievement. Not some nebulous phantasmagoria, but a real prospect which in our hearts we knew was possible of achievement. He did not scold us, he did not preach to us. He began the slow, tedious, and sometimes painful, process of 'raising our sights.' We needed the long view and he showed it to us."

Frank Graham, a student at the University of North Carolina when Weatherford brought him to leadership in the YMCA, a man who would eventually become the President of the University, United States Senator from North Carolina, and then a special mediator for the United Nations, has said: "There were no bounds to

Weatherford's energy and his devotion as he went from state to state and college to college. He had no patience with sloth, complacency, or low standards in religion, personal life, scholarship, athletics, and campus citizenship."

To secure thorough intellectual commitment to excellence on the part of his students, Weatherford realized that he would have to maintain the same standards himself. When he first started traveling such a wide territory, many people warned him that he would wither intellectually. Vowing that this should not happen, Weatherford formed a habit which would remain with him the rest of his life. He began to carry books in his brief case or satchel, and he read at least one each week. Later he would read two, three, four a week.

They were hard, driving years, those decades of the student secretaryship. Long, hot train rides (occasionally behind a wood-burning engine) led to stops at dreary little hotels. (At one university town there were two so-called hotels, and whichever one a visitor chose he wished he had gone to the other.) But Weatherford was proclaiming a new spiritual awareness and physical plenteousness to the youth of the South—and he found it a great time to live and work.

Eventually he made visits to colleges in every state in the union. One season he spoke to universities along the West Coast, from Seattle to Southern California. But during these early years there were also other interests. Love and death and a remarkable building project became part of his agenda.

6

Weatherford's concern was the whole person. A healthy mind in a healthy body, plus a strong spiritual commitment: this was the first ideal he sought not only for himself but also for all the young people with whom he came in contact.

A large measure of his appeal to youth grew from the fact that he did not concentrate, as many of his contemporary religious leaders did, upon eternity to the exclusion of the present. (After all, he seemed to be saying, if we cannot make fit use of the moments we have in this world, how shall we fulfill the possibilities of unlimited eons?) Search for beauty of the spirit did not exclude appreciation of more readily apparent physical beauty. (After all, if we cannot see and take joy in the tangible loveliness we encounter each day, how shall we be fully aware of it in more intangible realms?)

Rugged, forceful, hard-driving, here was a man who also cultivated a natural taste for what has euphemistically been called "the finer things of life," by which we often seem to suggest those adjuncts to daily living which we deem readily expendable. Actually, of course, they are not expendable at all.

The girl Weatherford had met while he was still a

student at Vanderbilt, Lula Belle Trawick, seemed to him beautiful. She was dainty and small-boned, wore her light brown hair coiled into a wispy crown above her gentle face. She played the violin, and "Traumerei" became one of Weatherford's favorite musical selections. In December, 1903, Weatherford and Lula Belle Trawick were married.

He had finished his first year and a quarter of strenuous work as International YMCA Student Secretary for the colleges of the South and Southwest. He was married to an exquisite wife. His confidence grew and so did his dreams.

One idea in particular was forming in his mind. When he was a boy his mother had told him of the tall North Carolina hills where she was born and reared. Willis was especially fascinated by stories of chestnut and chinquapin hunts each autumn when the ripe brown nuts lay thick as a carpet on the ground. There were no chestnut trees or chinquapin bushes on the Texas plains. He had seen something of that mountain country when he attended a Student YMCA Conference near Asheville, North Carolina, during the summer of 1903, and he longed to explore it more fully. Consequently, in 1904, the first summer after his marriage, he and his wife went to live for a season on the North Fork of the beautiful Swannanoa River in Western North Carolina.

J. L. M. Curry, renowned administrator of the Peabody Fund and advocate of the public school movement at the turn of the century, had married an Asheville woman and built a cabin in that part of the Swannanoa watershed known locally as the North Fork. The Weatherfords rented this cottage. Later in the summer Dr. O. E. Brown, one of the ablest professors Weatherford had known at Vanderbilt, and Mrs. Brown joined the Weatherfords for a vacation in this mountain valley.

That summer was one of the turning points in Weatherford's career. From that time on, Appalachia and all that concerned it was an indivisible part of his lifelong concern.

The only church in the valley was Baptist, and on their first Sunday Weatherford and his wife attended both Sunday School and church services. When Sunday School assembled, Weatherford saw six boys sitting apart without a teacher. He volunteered to teach them.

By the third Sunday Weatherford had rounded up most of the boys in the valley who were between twelve and fifteen years old and had enrolled them in his class. Then a delegation of men in the congregation came and asked him to preach for them. There were between thirty and forty families in the valley, and they had no regular pastor for their church. During the rest of the summer Weatherford conducted weekly services. He and his wife were invited to meals in practically every home.

With each new contact Weatherford looked more closely at the lives of these mountain people. Gradually he came to know and understand them. After all, he was akin to them through his parents and grandparents.

The patriarch of North Fork was Lafayette Burnett, known as "Fate," and through him and his family Weatherford caught a glimpse of the pioneer tradition as it persisted in these remote hills and hollows. Fate Burnett had been one of twelve children. He stood six feet and two inches tall and weighed about two hundred pounds. He and his six brothers had all fought for the Confederacy during the Civil War; four died on the battlefield. A son later described his "deep rumbling voice, ice-blue eyes and remarkable strength and temper."

His wife, "Aunt Sally" Allison Burnett, weighed less than a hundred pounds and was barely five feet tall. Whether or not she had been notified of his coming, Weatherford always felt welcome at her table. There she presided at the head of the board with a pitcher of milk, a pitcher of cream, and a pot of coffee in front of her, and her husband to her left. She ate so little that her husband often joked, "If Sally ever ate, I couldn't have afforded to keep her." Through this family, with their wide connections and frontier fondness for dogs, hunting, personal politics, and strong friendships, Weatherford and his wife became acquainted with a fundamental part of Appalachian life.

He responded warmly to the mountain people. He did not see them, as had so many journalists, missionaries, and other itinerant observers, as quaint repositories of folklore or cute hillbillies. They were individuals— indeed they were that!—and he respected their individuality.

Three days after he and his wife had arrived on North Fork, he asked one of the Burnett clan if he could buy some potatoes which he saw growing in the garden. When the man replied that he didn't have any potatoes, Weatherford did not grow angry or argue the issue. He simply waited. (He was a mountaineer, too—by genealogy and temperament if not by geography.) After his third Sunday in the pulpit, he again asked Burnett, "You surely have a few potatoes I could buy?" This time his neighbor replied, "There's plenty. But I won't sell them to you. Go on out and help yourself to all you want. There's a hoe in the patch!" It was a typical mountain response in both instances: the initial reticence toward unproved outsiders, the whole-hearted acceptance when the stranger proved his friendliness.

Weatherford's encounter with one of the children of the valley was a forerunner of many similar associations in later years. Quite a distance up on the mountain above the cabin the Weatherfords had rented lived a little girl who was an albino, so near-sighted that she could hardly see at all. The Weatherfords bought their dairy products from her family, walking to the farm each afternoon for fresh milk and butter. Weatherford succeeded in making friends with the other children of the family, but all overtures to the handicapped child were rejected. She was so shy that she would not allow the newcomer to come close enough to her to say a word before she bolted and ran like one of the rabbits in her father's pasture. Weatherford persisted in his efforts at friendship.

One afternoon when he went to the house, Miss Melissa, the girl's aunt, accompanied him to the nearby springhouse for his jug of milk. (Miss Melissa was so energetic that mountain neighbors compared her to "a four-horse team with a dog trotting under the wagon." In this respect she reminded Weatherford of his mother and sisters.) Presently the two of them heard a patter of feet on the path behind them, and in a moment the little girl dashed up to the springhouse bench near where Weatherford was standing, set down a small jar, and fled back up the path.

"That young'un has been after her mother all morning to let her give you that jar of preserves," Miss Melissa explained.

Then Weatherford knew that communication had been established even though no word had yet been exchanged between himself and this odd child.

A short while later he asked her mother if he might take the child to Asheville, some fifteen miles away, and have her eyes examined. They had to go by train, and she had never been on a train before. The oculist made the examination and fitted her with glasses. A minor miracle was wrought in this girl's life. She went to school. After she finished high school she enrolled at an excellent woman's college in Raleigh, North Carolina, from which she graduated. When she returned home she became head of her family and helped rear three younger children.

The summer spent in the little North Fork valley was a good one for the Weatherfords. As September and a new year of work in the colleges approached, Weatherford prepared to leave this community—but he had every intention of returning to the vicinity. There was something in these mountains, their wind-swept pinnacles, their folded valleys, their wide vistas and green forests, that he had found nowhere else: something uncorrupted, worthy of a man's efforts, inspiring a man to the best that was in him—something, in short, God-made rather than man-made.

He had found this good place, experienced this enrichment from the beauty of nature; logically, to him, the next question was, how could he share it with others? Especially, how could he bring this experience to those about whom he had come to care so fervently: the young men and women he met at all those institutions of higher learning throughout the region. He began to think about those summer conferences.

It has been recorded that the first interdenominational Christian conference held in the South was the Student Conference of the YMCA which met in 1892 at the University of Tennessee in Knoxville. In the twelve years following, it had assembled at various schools and even one resort hotel in the mountains. After a couple of seasons of personal experience with the shortcomings inherent in this arrangement, however, Weatherford commenced to lay plans for something more permanent.

John R. Mott came to speak at the student conference being held at the Asheville School for Boys. There were three hundred and sixty delegates present in buildings equipped to take care of some one hundred and twenty-five people. As Weatherford walked with Dr. Mott to the hillside conference grounds where the internationally famous leader was to address the open-air Sunday afternoon convocation, he told Mott of his dream of a

56

permanent conference home. "The way it is now," Weatherford protested, "we're stepchildren running from this place to that place. We need grounds and buildings of our own."

Mott agreed. Weatherford had expected that he would. He and Mott had met before, and from their first encounter each must have realized that he had met a personality that was in many ways akin to his own. There is little doubt that Mott was one of the decisive influences in Weatherford's adult life. Because of this influence, and the curious lack of knowledge among many people today about this remarkable man, perhaps a few facts about his career are relevant here.

Born in a country town in New York in 1865, Mott grew up in Iowa and went to Cornell University, where he became an outstanding student leader. Upon graduation he entered YMCA student work and from that time forward became one of the great international Christian leaders of his time. He was personal representative of the President of the United States on two important missions, author of thirteen books, holder of seven honorary degrees from some of the world's greatest universities, and recipient of awards and decorations from fifteen governments. In 1946 he was awarded the Nobel Peace Prize for his effort in improving "understanding between men."

In 1902, when John R. Mott had sent the telegram that brought Weatherford into student work, the two men met for the first time that summer at Northfield, Massachusetts. This was the big student conference of the Y, and here Weatherford heard Mott speak and came to know him personally. Weatherford decided that Mott was a man who knew what he wanted, plotted the road he would take to get it, and then attacked the problem with all his vigorous personality. If he was afflicted with doubts, no one else learned of them.

At that same conference Mott also discovered the younger man who had these same qualities to such a marked degree. When he asked Weatherford to come to his room and invited him to talk over plans for the coming year's work, he did not tell Weatherford what ought to be done. Instead he asked for ideas about visiting a college campus.

If Mott had expected to catch his new worker unprepared, he had underestimated his newest student secretary. Promptly and earnestly the young man began to lay out his plans for each visit. The saturation program of lectures, conferences, and travel was ambitious, but if John R. Mott questioned whether his young novice could carry through such a schedule, he gave no sign of his doubts.

Weatherford received no word of caution or discouragement from his organization's greatest leader then, and he did not receive it later when he broached the subject of a permanent summer conference center. Mott immediately understood the need, grasped what Weatherford wanted, and said he would cooperate fully in asking that the International Committee of the YMCA give Weatherford free time in which to raise money for such a center.

When the committee received the request, however, its members refused to grant Mott's wishes. They pointed to the heavy load of work Weatherford was already carrying. They felt that any other undertaking would dissipate his energy and effectiveness.

Weatherford was stunned by their refusal. He could not understand their blindness to the existing need, their short-sightedness to the opportunity. But he did not intend to be bound by their decision, for three reasons.

First, John R. Mott had encouraged him. Second, he had seen the mountains and the locale they offered for the place he envisioned. Third, he met every day the young people he wanted to enrich to the fullest of their capabilities. As a gesture of interest, the YMCA committee had sanctioned Weatherford's use of his summer vacation for the purpose of locating a conference site, if he wished to spend his free time this way. (A superfluous permission if ever there was one!) Of course, Weatherford wished to spend his time this way.

A judge in Asheville who had heard of Weatherford's idea told him that on a recent train ride into Asheville he had spotted an ideal location for such a building or buildings as Weatherford described. The site was on the slope of a mountain almost exactly opposite the North Fork valley where Weatherford and his wife had spent their first memorable Appalachian summer.

On October 6, 1906, a bright autumn day when the oaks and poplars, hickories and maples were brilliant with their reds and golds, Weatherford and a friend from Richmond, Virginia, Dr. A. L. Phillips of the Presbyterian Sunday School Board, drove in a hired buggy toward the hills east of Asheville. Near the village of Black Mountain they came to the property the judge had sighted: a tract of better than a thousand acres, most of it covered with timber, watered by clear pure springs.

The two men went deeper into the woods, trudged higher on the hillsides, and at last paused on a broad benchland overlooking the slopes below. Because the country around them was heavily wooded, the two men could not make out what the view might be if they chose this site. Weatherford spotted a tall oak tree. He climbed it and looked out. The rugged beauty of the highest peaks east of the Mississippi River and the green friendliness of the valley of the Swannanoa mingled in the panorama before him. This was the place where he would build a summer conference center to bring people experiences they would never forget.

He came down from the tree and began to plan. From a bank in Asheville, Weatherford and Phillips borrowed five thousand dollars, in their own names, to make a payment on 952 acres "more or less." They gave personal notes for the balance of the purchase price of $11,500. Then, in addition to his regular work, Weatherford set himself a new task.

The following spring he launched a project that seemed well-nigh impossible to many who knew him and the region. He set out to raise fifty thousand dollars for founding his permanent YMCA student training center. An official from national headquarters in New York was sent south to help in this initial drive for funds.

During long weary days and weeks the two men traveled and worked. The reception they received from businessmen, philanthropists, and organizations was pleasant but cool. Contributions were totally inadequate. After a month, the two men assessed their work one hot Sunday afternoon in a hotel room in Knoxville, Tennessee.

After a while the older man said, "Weatherford, we're not going to make it."

"No," the other agreed.

Startled at such ready acquiescence to failure, the official fund-raiser went on. "I'll go back to New York and report that we can't get fifty thousand."

"We can't raise fifty thousand," Weatherford said, "but we could five hundred thousand!"

His companion was really startled now.

"A project with only fifty thousand dollars invested in it can go out of existence any time and be forgotten overnight," Weatherford went on. "No wonder people don't want to put their money into something like that. If an undertaking is worth ten times that amount, it will be permanent. And people will be glad to take part in it."

The older hand was far from convinced of this high road to success. But neither was Weatherford convinced of their low road to failure. He proposed to go and see John D. Rockefeller, Senior, personally and present his case for the needs of Southern students and this center for their development.

A short while later, he did just that. Working through Starr Murphy, Rockefeller's lawyer, Weatherford received his first substantial gift toward his new half-million-dollar goal. That single gift was fifty thousand dollars.

With this plan Weatherford had outstripped even John R. Mott, who was noted for his big dreams. Mott had visualized buying fifty acres, putting up one building with an auditorium and dining room, and then using tents to accommodate the five or six hundred college boys who would meet there, all at a cost of fifty thousand dollars.

With ten times as large a goal, Weatherford bought a total of 1,585 acres of North Carolina mountain land and began planning a great white-columned structure that would be named Lee Hall, a landmark in more ways than one, and the center of the Blue Ridge Assembly.

During this construction his work load was heavier than ever, but stiff challenges had always exhilarated rather than exhausted him. Besides, there was an extra reason for jubilant faith and effort now. His young wife was expecting a baby. To someone who had always cared so intensely about other people's children, this promise of one of his own brought special content.

Then, in June, 1907, as their baby was struggling to be born, his wife died. The diagnosis was uremic poisoning. For a brief time the orderly, purposeful personal world Weatherford had created reeled around him. He had come from a hardy people endowed with strong physiques and long lives. Except for his own dangerous youthful bout with typhoid and the death of his high school classmate from tuberculosis, he had had scant experience of serious illness or death. Now the little family he had made central in his affections and his dreams for the future were suddenly swept away. He was alone in a way he had never known before.

Work seemed to be all that was left to Weatherford now, and for a while he sought it as a refuge where once it had been a fulfillment. Perhaps it was at this time too that he learned the words of his favorite mountain ballad:

> *We must walk this lonely valley,*
> *We must walk it all alone,*
> *Nobody else can walk it for us,*
> *We must walk it for ourselves.*

7

"Suffering is surely a basis for human understanding," Weatherford once wrote. He pointed out that "the basic fact lying behind all pain is sensitivity. If we were not sensitive, we would not have pain, and the higher we develop in the plane of life, the more sensitive we grow. You can judge a man's growth of soul by how sensitive he is to wrong or evil. To make us insensitive would be to destroy life."

Weatherford underwent the ordeal of his personal sorrow by choosing sensitivity rather than callousness, by permitting it to enlarge his sympathy for the trials of others rather than encouraging retreat into bitterness over his own loss. He carried on with his work, and now he brought to it a compassion which only experience could provide. He saw anew a poverty of that compassion in many around him.

During the next few years he began to travel outside the South. Between his work at the colleges and his labor toward building the assembly at Blue Ridge, he went to visit his mother, his older sister Flora, and his brother Robert, who lived in Arizona. He visited the Grand Canyon and camped in its depths. He stood beside the Colorado River and contemplated its energy and the results of its persistence.

He also went abroad to meetings in England and on the Continent where he spoke in public, and in private he made it a point to become acquainted with as wide a cross section of people as he could. Problems of the South, to which he always returned, were clarified when seen in perspective, and he became increasingly sensitive to the lives of those who were imprisoned by the poverty of mind and body that bred ignorance and prejudice.

The South was afflicted with many poverties at this time. The estimated per capita wealth in the United States was $1,950. In the South it was half as much, $993. What did this mean in terms of daily life? For one thing it meant that while the average expenditure for each school-age child was $2.84 for the country as a whole, in Florida and Texas, for instance, it was $1.46 and in Alabama and North Carolina only 50 cents! While an average school term in most of the United States was 145 days, in the South it was 100 days. Less than 40 per cent of the potential school population attended school regularly, and the average value of school buildings in the region was $276.

What did poverty of cash mean in terms of the health of people? Although public health programs were developing, malaria, hookworm, and pellagra took a terrible toll in the health and energy of large segments of the population. Child labor, especially in the cotton mills, was an entrenched evil so widely accepted that although, as one historian has pointed out, "by 1912 all Southern states had adopted an age-and-hour limit and some sort of prohibition against night work for children; in the leading textile states the age limit was still only twelve and the hours sixty a week. An investigation by the Federal Bureau of Labor revealed that the age-limit laws were 'openly and freely violated in every State visited,' that out of 143 mills in five Southern states, 107 employed children under 12 years of age illegally."

On the farms, tenants of the single crop, cotton, were often almost as much in bondage as the slaves a few decades earlier. A survey, *How Farm Tenants Live*, published in 1922 by the University of North Carolina, revealed that in two North Carolina counties the average income for white farm-owners was 34 cents a day; for Negro farm-owners, 32 cents. For black renters it was 16 cents per day, and for white renters 14 cents. Negro sharecroppers averaged 10 cents a day, and white sharecroppers—lowest men on the totem pole—8 cents a day! It became a proverb that tenancy and illiteracy went hand in hand.

"Only the beneficent climate and the merciful creditor who extends a few 'pantry' supplies make life possible in these circumstances," the survey concluded. "Such poverty is deadening. It places all cultural things beyond reach. Conveniences, necessities even, decent clothing, shoes, proper tools, the services of doctors and dentists, are frequently not within the tenant families' possibilities. Material poverty is wedded to spiritual numbness."

With the 20-20 vision that hindsight boasts, we do not find it hard today to muster horror at such conditions and to advance solutions for them. Solutions were complicated by many factors, however, and two of the most important were the Northern capital that financed and profited from many of these conditions, and the presence of the Negro that compounded every economic, political, and social problem with the emotional and easily exploited overtones of race.

As Weatherford traveled the South there were others traveling, too, disseminating quite different messages. He arrived at one South Carolina college the day after the famous governor and senator, "Pitchfork Ben" Tillman, had held forth on the platform. The stock in trade of this demagogue was race-baiting, and while he controlled his state's politics for a generation, his influence spread to many other areas.

Between 1901 and 1909 Tillman made countless speeches in all parts of the United States, discovering ready audiences for his tirades against "the ignorant and debased and debauched black race." On this particular occasion the college president told Weatherford he might speak to the students a full hour instead of the customary fifteen minutes. In this request there was an unspoken comment on the political poison they had been exposed to the preceding day, for Weatherford spoke in direct opposition to all that Tillman had propounded. The South as a whole, of course, listened far too long to its Tillmans rather than to its Weatherfords, to the impoverishment of everyone.

In April, 1908, Weatherford brought seven Southern leaders together in Atlanta to discuss the racial situation. He had become acutely aware of the inequities in health, education, justice, and opportunity that held the Negro in the ditch and, as his friend Booker T. Washington had warned, kept the Southern white man there with him. He had become aware of the fact that while the life expectancy for a white man was fifty years, for a Negro man it was thirty-four years. Simply by being born black he had lost some sixteen years of precious life. He had also greatly increased his chances of death by violence. In 1908 there were ninety-three Negroes lynched. And beyond these flesh-and-blood statistics there were the shacks huddled together in the Negro portions of the towns and cities Weatherford visited, the rural hovels spread across the countryside he traversed, and these spoke in eloquent silence to his conscience.

When he asked these seven men to meet in Atlanta, he hoped that they might address themselves to the special consideration of what white college men of the South might do to improve the racial situation.

Two aspects of this conference are especially notewor-thy. First, at a time when any public contact between the races which might suggest equality was frowned upon or forbidden outright, Weatherford's meeting brought together four Negroes and three whites to look at a common problem. Weatherford did not believe any situation could be understood or permanently im-proved without participation by those most centrally in-volved. Second, the conference proposed to discover no "solution" to the big question it admitted, but it did pro-pose search for specific improvements to specific portions of that question.

The difficulties of "a solution" to this thorniest of all the nation's domestic dilemmas were forcefully stated by an advanced sociologist of the South writing at about this time. He said, "Neither dogmatism nor emotion is very helpful in a difficult situation; and, above all, the negro problem is a difficult problem. In fact, it is not one but a thousand and one problems; and there is no clear-cut formula and no magic rule. There is no solu-tion. . . . All that may be asked for is a change in the relative position of some of the factors, for the problem, as a problem, remains in a new form—possibly under a new name—but it remains, and taxes the ingenuity of man to a greater subtlety and more finesse.

"How much more evenly the world would go if honest men could learn to know that there are really two kinds of solutions—the possible and the impossible, and that the impossible ones are no solution at all. An impossible formula is a kind of emotional substitute for a facing of the facts. It is an escape from the problem. The real reason so much energy is expended in behalf of the im-possible is because the possible is difficult and incon-venient."

Once Weatherford accepted a problem as his own, he shouldered the difficulties and inconveniences of facing it practically, however. As for the seven men who met that April day, each was eminent in either the religious or educational world. After six hours of thorough and candid conference it became evident that ignorance of the basic facts of Southern Negro life was the first hurdle to be overcome.

Dr. W. R. Lambuth, of the Southern Methodist Episcopal Church, said, "We need a book, Weatherford, setting forth the situation. Why don't you write it for us?"

Dr. John Hope, President of the Negro Atlanta Baptist College, later part of Atlanta University, agreed as did the others in the group. Weatherford added one more task to his work load.

He launched into research for this book with characteristic zeal. He drew on available data concerning economic conditions, health and housing, educational and religious life of the Negro, but he was not satisfied that statistics conveyed the substance of the story. He went to look for himself. He interviewed extensively and drew some personal conclusions from information gathered by his eyes, ears, nose, and mouth in a variety of places. He was appalled at some of the conditions he discovered.

He learned that in an Alabama school for white girls only a short while before, a malignant epidemic of typhoid fever had broken out. A number of girls died; many more were in bed for weeks and months. An exhaustive search traced the infection to a Negro boy who worked in the kitchen and who was described by the bacteriologist as "a walking arsenal of typhoid germs." How, Weatherford wondered and asked, could relatives of those dead girls ever feel again that the race problem did not concern them?

In North Carolina he discovered that the average cost of Negro public school buildings was $124.37. Only 64 out of 2,198 of these schools had any desks. For the rest there were benches. In 30 counties of the state, where there were nearly 60,000 Negro children of school age, teachers in the country schools were paid an average of less than seventeen dollars a month.

One South Carolina alley Weatherford encountered was lined with thirty-two Negro tenement houses, and the sole supply of water was "an open dipping well surrounded by a sixteen-inch curb. On this curb all the people of the thirty-two houses do their washing, etc." No wonder he found that of every two Negro babies born in this city only one lived to be a year old.

"This," he said, "is a death plague almost like that visited upon the children of Egypt by the destroying angel."

In 1910, *Negro Life in the South*, the product of his research and concern, was published. This was the first of five books he would write on race relations.

The small volume became a landmark, not because its contents were a definitive study of the subject, which they were not, nor because its liberal tone had divested itself of all echoes of Southern paternalism, which it had not, but because it forthrightly stated that white men must look at black men and see the interrelationship of their co-existence. It set forth some of the realities of the daily life of Negroes in the South.

It was also a landmark because it stated, in conclusion, "It is not the negro that is on trial before the world, but it is we, the white men of the South." This was one of the earliest statements of such responsibility. Most Southerners, most Americans, most of the white race would not become aware of this, nor admit it, for fully another generation and longer.

Another fact Weatherford understood and pointed out in this book in 1910 still plagues us today: "What we need more than any other one element in our Southern industrial life is trained laborers. There are eight million negroes in our very midst; the graduates of Hampton and Tuskegee have forever dispelled the doubt that they can be made efficient workmen by proper training; when will there be enough of constructive study and statesmanship in the South to harness this mighty force and make it the wonder of the world in its wealth producing power?"

There would not be enough statesmanship for many years to come. Yet Weatherford's labors were not in vain. During the next few years, 30,000 copies of his book were studied by more than 50,000 students. The book's deepest impact—on individual attitudes and understanding—could not be measured, of course. There were, however, some apparent results.

Some of the students who studied *Negro Life in the South* organized discussion groups in their schools and tried to discover practical ways in which they might help improve the lives around them. In at least one university a group of students went to a neighborhood Negro church where they assembled classes and taught Negro boys and men to read and write. For four years while they were at college they worked to raise the literacy level of the nearby Negro community.

There were other examples of direct action taken by white students whose previous attitudes often had arisen more out of poverty of vision to conditions around them than out of poverty of feeling to the harshness of those conditions. In fact, some of those who studied this and other early books by Weatherford were directly led to devote their lives to social concerns and labors.

Eugene Barnett, international YMCA leader who spent the major portion of his life in the Orient, wrote in 1956: "By now the lists have been entered by a multitude of champions of humane, just and brotherly relations among the races in these United States, but some of us remember when Weatherford was a rather lonely pioneer in that championship. Characteristically he

70

sought out the facts in the case, set them forth in books and articles where they could be read and studied, and through the College Associations engaged the minds, the consciences and the activity of Christian men."

There were other Southern liberals of this period, many of them more famous than Weatherford. But almost without exception they became liberals-in-exile. Many of them took up residence in New York or Boston or other metropolitan centers. Their forums were usually newspapers and magazines, college campuses, or philanthropic foundations outside the South. This was, of course, perfectly legitimate and often necessary as a means of sheer self-preservation. The fact remains, however, that Weatherford stuck it out in the South. The demagogues might rant and rave and assume a season of power in part of the region. Poverty might blight the potential of whole segments. Indifference and apathy might seem to smother every flickering flame that was lit in a corner of the region. But Weatherford was a product of the South, too. He was as tough as the demagogues, as tenacious as the poverty and apathy. Most important, he was working for something larger than himself. He had caught a vision of the plenteousness that was possible for the South whenever it would throw off its self-inflicted shackles.

While others were spending their lives and investing their capital in the lands or mills or mines or factories of the New South, Weatherford was investing in the human resources. An assistant secretary of labor for our federal government wrote an article in 1964, "Poverty and Progress," in which he said, "Perhaps the major social discovery of the postwar period has been . . . in demonstrating that investment in human capital—*not* physical capital, *not* technology—is the major source of contemporary economic growth." W. D. Weatherford had come to that conclusion more than fifty years earlier.

8

On February 6, 1912, Governor Ben W. Hooper of Tennessee issued a call for a meeting to be termed the Southern Sociological Congress. He requested the governors of fifteen other Southern states to cooperate with him in developing the agenda and creating a congress which would prove useful and effective.

There were fundamental social conditions aplenty which cried out for leadership, for sheer humane citizenship. These included a barbarous chain gang and prison code which allowed indignities of the most sadistic nature, child labor practices which winked at long working hours and pennies of pay for children who were virtually slaves, racial proscriptions which condoned peonage and flagrant injustices of law. In addition there were, of course, the constant problems of schools, health, housing, and labor for all the people in a region that was, in many ways, the stepchild of the rest of the country.

A committee was appointed to organize this Congress, and its object was to bring together representative people from the entire South who were interested in social welfare. Together they would study ways to improve specific situations. The Congress met from May 7 to May 10. Delegates from twenty-eight states, the District of

Columbia, Canada, and Africa brought total attendance to about seven hundred.

At this Congress W. D. Weatherford discussed "The Negro and the New South." No topic under survey at that meeting was more explosive. What Weatherford had to say at that time about a Negro minority is important to record because it is, in almost every aspect, equally pertinent today when applied to an Appalachian minority people or to any of those small groups or nations anywhere in the world where larger nations and technological forces have power to subvert human values for material gain.

In that year of 1912 sixty-one Negroes were lynched. In the dozen years since the turn of the century 1,010 Negroes had died by lynching. This is more than a brutal statistic. It is a revelation of the attitude of the society which would permit it, a society in which contempt of every sort, from the smallest discourtesy to the most foul infamy, was the daily lot of the Negro. Worse, this was accepted as the normal attitude, as the Southern way of life, as it were, by the majority of white people. Against this background of blunted sensibilities and accepted injustices, Weatherford spoke in Nashville.

After summarizing some of the strides the South had made since the Civil War and its devastating aftermath, he said: "Yes, we are living in a New South. But economic and intellectual improvement do not make a people great. They are a background and basis for greatness, but they are not the essence of greatness. While we are great in these lines, there is another realm in which we are to make progress if we are to attain greatness. The test of an individual or a nation is not in the realm of possession nor in the realm of knowledge, but in the realm of relationships. It is not what we have or what we know that makes us great, but our attitude toward humanity."

Touching the problems of child labor and the penal system and other subjects the Congress had under consideration, Weatherford went on to say: "A Congress like this has absolutely no meaning save in so far as we attach sacredness and value to personality. And when you say personality that means all personality; it means the bad as well as the good, it means the defective as well as the efficient, it means the unattractive as well as the attractive, it means the diseased as well as the physically sound—yes, more than all these, it means the black as well as the white. If it does not mean this, then this Congress is a mere mockery, and we, as delegates, are sham men and women trying to play at make-believe interest in humanity."

Weatherford had practiced his public speaking well in that schoolroom back in Weatherford, Texas. He had received his conviction on the frontiers of rural Methodism at its crusading best. These had been buttressed by years of systematic study in philosophy. All his fluency and faith and reason were brought to bear in this presentation.

"Immanuel Kant, in his *Critique of Practical Reason*," Weatherford told his listeners, "lays down this maxim: 'So act as to treat humanity, whether in thine own person or in that of any other, in every case as an end withal, never as a means.' The most serious danger of the South today is that we shall, on this very Negro question, lose our valuation of humanity, as such, because we want to use the Negro as a tool for our own comfort.

"The question is whether we will be interested in him as a person, as a being worthy in himself, as an end, or whether we will value him simply and solely as a hewer of wood and a drawer of water, and that wood and that water for the white man's use alone.

"The supreme race question, therefore, is not one of efficiency or inefficiency alone, it is not one of advance-

ment or lack of advancement, it is one of personal attitude. An Old South cannot become a New South until
every man, woman and child in that South has a value
as a person, and not simply as a thing, as an economic
tool or a piece of animal machinery."

Half a century later he would extend that warning
against man used as an economic tool or a piece of
machinery to include the human crisis in industry. Perhaps this link between two great issues in contemporary
American life illustrates most clearly the fact that
Weatherford has concerned himself with the fundamental issues of our society. His philosophic and religious conviction of the sacredness of persons, all persons,
has kept him in the avant-garde in defense of the value
of personality, whether the destruction of that value is
racial bigotry or technological revolution.

The success of the first Sociological Congress in Nashville led to a second assembly in 1913 in Atlanta, and
a third in Memphis in 1914. This last time the Congress
met in conjunction with the National Conference of
Charities and Correction (later to become the National
Conference on Social Welfare). The joint sessions led
to conflict over racial policies.

The Congress had a number of Negro dues-paying
members. Weatherford, who was Chairman of the Committee on Organization as well as Secretary of the Committee on Race Relations, felt that they should be
included in all official activities on an equal basis with
other delegates. The best way to accomplish this, he
felt, was simply to go ahead and present the Congress
with a *fait accompli* when they came to the first night's
meeting. Consequently, Negroes were not segregated;
they sat on the first floor of the auditorium during the
initial gathering.

Early the next morning a group of Memphis businessmen called on Weatherford to protest this breach of

75

custom. For two hours they discussed the situation. Presently one of the officers of the Congress arrived, and the delegation asked him what he was going to do in answer to their protest. "Why," he replied, "I'm going to follow the lead of you Southern gentlemen."

Nothing he could have chosen to say would have angered Weatherford more. This attitude assumed that no bona-fide Southern gentleman ever questioned segregation or the accepted racial patterns of a community. Like the fiery Andy Jackson he admired so keenly, Weatherford was not one who accepted slurs—real or imagined—on his gentility.

Face flushed and eyes flashing, Weatherford turned on his colleague and demanded, "*I'm* a Southern gentleman, sir. Why don't you follow *my* lead?"

The upshot was that the issue was sent to a committee. Before the committee ruled, however, it was time for the second night's meeting. This session was directed by the National Conference of Charities and Correction, which decided that it should be segregated. The Negro delegates walked out of the meeting.

The next morning Weatherford met with the committee on arrangements and told them that the Sociological Congress would not segregate its Negro members on the third night when it was again to have its alternate turn in charge of the program. The local committee would not agree to this. They argued that the owner of the theater building where these sessions were being held would not permit such freedom of seating. Weatherford then told the committee he did not wish to embarrass them and so the Congress would change its meeting place to the First Methodist Church.

One of the church hierarchy, along with an influential editor of a Memphis newspaper, called upon Weatherford. Weatherford, still rankling under that "Southern gentleman" allusion and the embarrassment of seeing his Negro friends walk out of the convention the night before, stated his position with no little vigor. The editor turned to the church leader and said, "I think we should let them do what they think right and wise."

Weatherford wrote an announcement about the transfer of meeting places and the reason for the change. The crowd, both white and Negro, attending the program that night was the largest one the Congress had yet enjoyed. It took place at a time when Jim Crow laws in the South were at their tightest. Weatherford's victory for an unsegregated meeting won him friends among Negro leaders who remained his staunch supporters throughout their lives. He had buttressed his words with actions. One who never forgot this little incident was Robert Russa Moton, a great Negro educator and leader.

Weatherford had also proved to himself something he wished hesitant white liberals might have understood: "You can do many progressive things, take forward steps, if you just go ahead and do them, take them, seize the opportunity. It's hesitation, lack of conviction on your own part, that often kills an action and thwarts success."

In his address to the Sociological Congress that year Weatherford bore down heavily on the theme of the interdependence of all the region's people. "We are not eight million Negroes and twenty-one million whites," he said. "We are twenty-nine million human beings, and whatever affects one of our company must of necessity affect all the other 28,999,999. The sin of the immoral will destroy the safety of the moral, the disease of the weakest will destroy the health of the strongest, the prejudice of the most ignorant will warp the judgment of the most learned, the lawlessness of the most criminal will blacken the name and drag into criminal action the law-abiding instincts of the highest citizens. We must stand or fall together. Thank God this is true! This insures that the learned shall not despise the ignorant, that the physically sound shall not despise the physically weak, the rich man cannot scorn the poverty-stricken, the righteous cannot become self-righteous in their contempt for the morally weak. Every welfare movement for whites must become a welfare movement for Negroes as well. This interest in the whole will keep us from dying with the dry rot of complacency."

The year of the first Southern Sociological Congress Weatherford also published another book on the race question: *Present Forces in Negro Progress.* Forward steps in its author's own thinking were evident in this second volume. As a small but not unimportant illustration, he used the capital "N" for the word "Negro" in this second book; the word had not been capitalized anywhere in his first book. Aware that this was a startling innovation at the time, he carefully instructed the printer to follow the manuscript in every detail. When galley proofs of the book arrived and upper case "N's" had been set in lower case type, Weatherford told the printer to reset the whole book *the way it had been written.*

Even the most liberal Southern newspapers and their editors would not be printing "Negro" with a capital "N" for decades to come. Weatherford's insistence on this symbol of courtesy and dignity was an example of his stubbornness at its most constructive.

One notable section of Weatherford's second book discussed Southern farming and Negroes. Since the majority of Negroes in the region were tied to the land in one way or another, and since its agriculture was a key to the whole structure of Southern life at that time, Weatherford's insight and frank discussion were highly relevant.

He pointed out facts that sociologists and economists a quarter of a century later would discover and discuss with considerable erudition. For example, he said that "the three arch enemies of Southern farm life today are the tenant system, which appears under various guises; the one crop system, which continues to do what it did during slavery—eat up the land and leave it worthless; and lastly, that form of isolation which cheats the rural dweller out of his birthright of culture, growth and enjoyment. All of these evils bear more heavily on the average Negro than on the white man in the country."

Weatherford had gone out into the countryside of the South and looked, and questioned, and learned. One of the things he learned was that "the fight which many an obscure Negro farmer is making in order to buy his land is splendid beyond the belief of the average white man." He gave one small personal illustration.

"I was driving in Nottoway County, Virginia, and came upon a place owned by a Negro named Moses Fitzgerald. I went out into the field where he was at work, and found him barefooted harrowing and sowing clover. I learned something of his simple life story. Born a slave, starting with nothing, he began as a boy to trap rabbits and sell them for fifteen cents each and the hides for three cents each. In this way he accumulated enough to buy his first little plot, on which he began farming, saving scrupulously every penny, until now he owns one hundred and fifty-five acres, has built a good five-room house, has a good team, and sends his children to school."

Weatherford was not content simply to bring out such individual instances of work and thrift and success. He called for an end to the stereotype of Negroes as shiftless and lazy. After his book was published he went to the United States Secretary of Agriculture and discussed the possibility of sending his study to the farm demonstration agents of every county in the South and Southwest.

He was convinced, through his own observations and interviews, that Negro farmers were more eager for help and more amenable to instructions than many white farmers. There was great need for more farm agents who were either Negro themselves or who would work with Negro farmers. Weatherford pointed out that, according to census reports in 1910, Negroes were cultivating—either as owners, tenants, or hired laborers—one hundred million acres of land.

"If," he said, "farm demonstration work can double the yield of these millions of acres, the white people of the South will be stupid indeed if they do not insist that these Negro farmers be given a full chance. Here is the opportunity for the white farm demonstrator to prove that he is a democrat indeed, and believes in an equal chance for all by helping his Negro neighbor."

The secretary of agriculture agreed to send the book to Southern farm demonstration agents if Weatherford could find financing for the project. The secretary's office would lend only its prestige and approval to the undertaking.

Weatherford then went to Chicago and sought out Julius Rosenwald, head of Sears-Roebuck, whose Rosenwald Fund would become famous for the rural Negro schools it built across the South and for its other contributions to alleviating racial problems. Weatherford presented a picture of the Southern farm situation to Rosenwald, then proposed that his book might be of practical help to Negro farmers. Farm demonstrators, Weatherford explained to Rosenwald, were United States employees who worked with a number of individuals in each community to show improved farming results by use of better fertilizers and methods of cultivation and varieties of seeds. If these demonstrators could read Weatherford's book, they might be aroused to work with more Negroes. Rosenwald agreed to finance this project of sending *Present Forces in Negro Progress* to Southern farm demonstration agents. It was a grass-roots educational effort.

It is pointless to argue today that these agricultural leaders should have been seeing the needs and handicaps which beset Negro farmers every day in the fields. It is equally pointless to speculate on what might have been accomplished for the economy of the South and nation if full knowledge and adoption of improved farming techniques could have been extended to all the South's people at this early date. Our purpose here is to record the fact that in a time when too few leaders faced up to the truism that "poor people make poor land," and vice versa, Weatherford was putting forth practical effort to improve the basic agricultural knowledge of the lowest Southerners on the economic totem pole.

Weatherford continued to believe that education was the prime force capable of transforming the South's poverty into the plenty that its human and natural riches seemed to warrant. Educational needs in the South at this time were vast indeed.

Historian Louis R. Harlan, documenting what those needs were in the years between 1901 and 1915, has described the situation succinctly: "The educational problem was not a single one, but rather a complex of social problems. Antiquated and poorly furnished one-room schools in two separate systems were taught by poorly trained and poorly paid teachers. Funds must come from the self-taxation of a poor people hampered by the inertia of a political machine linked with propertied interests hostile to taxation. Antagonism between the white and the Negro masses could be utilized by opponents of increased expenditure for universal education."

In South Carolina the average expenditure in 1915 was $16.22 for each white child enrolled in school and $1.93 for each Negro child.

Dr. Harlan has cited one Southern newspaper which stated quite clearly a widely held viewpoint on the uses of education for Negroes: "Education has but one tendency: to give higher hopes and aspirations. There can be but one result in educating the negro [sic]. . . . We want the negro to remain here, just about as he is—with mighty little change. We want them to become better cooks, better servants, better wash women, better workmen in farm and field and shop. We will cheerfully pay taxes to give him that sort of schooling . . . . Of course if the negro don't like this he can leave."

Weatherford would have agreed wholeheartedly with the editorialist's first sentence. It was precisely those "higher hopes and aspirations" that he labored to arouse in all Southerners: agricultural agents, tenant farmers, white, Negro, and especially young people. When he completed Blue Ridge Assembly and opened it for its first season of classes, lectures, and recreation, he hoped that it might become an intellectual Mecca for students of all ages and, eventually, of all races.

9

In the summer of 1912 Blue Ridge Assembly was ready
for its first season of conferences. Lee Hall, a white frame
structure with a broad porch fronted by a row of eight
stately columns three stories tall, large enough to accommodate more than three hundred people, sat on the
side of the mountain Weatherford had bought.

No, it did not sit on the side of the mountain so much
as it fitted into the slope of the mountain. Seen from the
highway, it nestled like a gleaming white mansion
among green trees and shrubs and the unspoiled beauty
of its natural surroundings. At one corner of the building
stood the oak tree that Weatherford had climbed the
memorable October day when he had located this site.

Even the road leading up to the hall, a curving, sweeping drive Weatherford had laid out himself with a hand
level and wooden stakes, was not visible from the highway. Guests who sat in the comfortable rocking chairs
on the veranda of Lee Hall looked out upon a majestic
view of the valley below and high ranges opposite. The
Craggies and the Blacks and numerous lesser peaks
loomed on the horizon, among the most rugged mountains of the Appalachian chain.

Weatherford had lavished care and enthusiasm on

building this place, on making it large enough, situating it at just the right spot on the mountain, panelling its reception-auditorium hall with cherry cut from these very acres, securing to it all the beauty and usefulness possible. Why?

He wanted this to be a place where the beauty of the mountains, woods, seasons—earth's bounty—could be seen first-hand and appreciated. Poverty of mind and spirit could be transformed, Weatherford hoped, by exposure to the grandeur of these wild natural surroundings, by experience of real educational effort, and by encounter with some of the finest leaders and speakers in the country. He hoped to accomplish this transformation especially for the staff that would do the work each summer at Blue Ridge.

Before he had begun to clear an acre of ground or lay the foundations for a single building, Weatherford made careful and definite plans and formulated certain goals. First, he would try to make at least one hundred students each year a little more alert and intellectually aware of the meaning of religion.

Second, Blue Ridge would exemplify in its own philosophy and actions a belief in the sacredness of all human personality.

Here, too, everyone would participate in the responsibility and joy of creative labor. Weatherford had come to believe that the experience of slavery had left a deep psychological scar on the South and its attitude toward work. He reasoned that the slave hated labor because it branded him as inferior, and the white man shunned labor because he thought it was the slave's province. Weatherford wanted to raise up a new generation who believed that any task which added richness to human existence was a sacred task.

In addition, every young person chosen to come to Blue Ridge as a member of its staff would have to show himself to be intellectually responsible. By this Weatherford meant to sift out the "loafers and floaters," as he labeled them—those he had seen at the colleges he visited who were scornful of genuine academic achievement and excellence. (The "Gentleman's C" was a fighting phrase to Weatherford.)

Finally, for a balanced life, quiet and meditation should be made part of each day. At Blue Ridge he hoped everyone would find time and inclination to be alone.

Summers at Blue Ridge were to be not only study of life, but experience of life as well.

Before the beginning of the first season Weatherford wrote to the presidents of thirty Southern women's colleges and told them he would like to have two of the most outstanding students from each school come to Blue Ridge that summer. He told the presidents: "These girls must have a B or better average in their studies. They must be active workers in some campus religious organization. And it won't hurt a bit if they're pretty!"

The same rules held true for boys applying to Blue Ridge for summer work—with the possible exception of the last qualification. One hundred college girls and boys were chosen. Weatherford was delighted when they arrived and he had a chance to look over his group. They seemed to him to be the very flower of Southern youth.

The first night of the summer session he did as he would do during subsequent years: he spoke to his boys and girls in the main reception room of Lee Hall before the big stone fireplace. He told them that he meant to work them harder than they had ever been worked before—and make them like it. That he achieved this goal over the years is demonstrated by the fact that after that first summer there were usually some one thousand applicants annually from all parts of the South who were eager to fill the one hundred openings.

Only college juniors and seniors were chosen. Of these,

almost half took one of Weatherford's courses. They usually complained about the hard study. The legend even flourished that Dr. Weatherford assigned half of the library volumes for collateral reading during each summer. But they urged those who came after them to take his courses.

He was a strict grader. As he had discovered in Lomax's course at Weatherford College, no paper could be perfect. But beyond the discipline of close, just grading was Weatherford's personal desire to make his favorite subject, the philosophy of religion, important to his young listeners. He could not tolerate what he felt was a sloppy attitude on the part of many people toward any religious thought or church work. He felt that discipline and growth and education of the spirit were no less important than education in physics, world literature, or a laboratory science.

It was not only study of relationships that Weatherford sought, however, and it was not only theorizing about the dignity of labor that he set forth. He brought both into the reality of daily practice. Many of his students, brought up under a completely different set of values and mores, later recalled that this experience marked a turning point in their lives. Practice as well as preaching of lofty sentiments brought almost daily small crises at Blue Ridge.

For example, no student was allowed to say "nigger," and yet some of the young people from the Deep South had never heard any other term. One summer a student from a Florida university was assigned to work as baggage man at Blue Ridge. This meant that he operated the hand-pulled elevator for trunks of the guests attending various conferences. At the end of the first two weeks the boy came to Weatherford's office. "My work is nigger's work," he protested.

Weatherford told him, "You had better change your

attitude toward both work and Negroes—or leave Blue Ridge. We respect both here."

On another occasion a girl came with a delegation of ten from a state teacher's college in Virginia. She was not one of the summer student work staff, but a member of a conference group meeting at Blue Ridge. On the way to the conference she lost her purse which contained her return train ticket and all her money. The other girls with her asked Weatherford to give her work so that she could earn her room and board and stay on for the meeting she had planned to attend. Weatherford already had his full work force, but he sympathized with the girl's dilemma and so he assigned her a table to serve in the dining room.

At noon he went to the dining room to check on the new waitress and see that everything was all right. He found the table he had assigned her unattended. When he searched her out, he discovered that she was in her room crying. Weatherford asked her what was wrong. "I just can't do it," she answered.

"Can't do what?" Weatherford wanted to know.

"I can't serve a table. That is what niggers do in my home."

Gently (for he knew the strength of the tradition which had marked her), yet firmly (for he knew the necessities of the present world opening around her), Weatherford explained to this girl that any labor which served a human being's needs was sacred and worthwhile. He also told her that the word "Negro" was spelled with a capital "N" and did not have two "gg's" or an "i" in it.

This Virginia girl dried her eyes and heard what Weatherford was trying to tell her. She met the challenge and served her table and served it well for the remainder of her visit at Blue Ridge.

Eventually they dubbed themselves P.W.G.'s and

P.W.B.'s, Poor Working Girls and Poor Working Boys, these young Southerners who came to the mountains and did work such as they had not tried before, heard truths they had not heard before, experienced religion such as they had not known existed before. They became participants in a sort of fellowship that was exclusive only in its breadth and depth and intensity.

Beyond their revised attitudes toward work and other races, there was also Weatherford's emphasis on meditation. He dramatized the need for quiet by taking small groups to a mountain top when the evenings were fine. There he made them sit in silence until the sun went down, for fifteen, twenty, thirty minutes. Many had never been on a hilltop or experienced a time of utter stillness before.

Thus Blue Ridge began its existence in 1912. That was an auspicious summer for its slim, energetic, practical and visionary president-director. He was thirty-six years old and he carried a heavy work load; there seemed to be no unfilled moment nor spare corner in his life. Yet he was lonely. The great personal devotion of which he was capable lay in him unused.

Among the hundred students who came to Blue Ridge from the best colleges of the South in that first summer was a tall, slender girl from Winthrop College in South Carolina. She was secretary of the YWCA there. Her name was Julia McCrory and she was a native of Alabama. There was something about her. . . .

Weatherford looked at her twice as she came into his office to talk about her work assignment and studies for the summer.

Was it her eyes? Someone later described them: "Her eyes were intensely blue—and always so wide open, as if she expected to see something special."

Was it the mixture of gentleness and gaiety, girlish charm coupled with a mature lady's reserve that set her apart from the others who had come to Blue Ridge?

Perhaps it was all of these and more—an unusually happy marriage of body, mind, and spirit in one person —that drew Willis Weatherford to Julia McCrory. Blue Ridge, over the years, would bring him many rewards and satisfactions, but no other gift as precious as Julia, his "dear girl" for a lifetime.

10

During the Christmas season after their first meeting at Blue Ridge, Weatherford went to Alabama to visit Julia. She lived in the country on a cotton plantation with her father. As a child she had had an unusually lonely life. A younger brother had died while he was small, and she had grown up as an only child. When she was nine years old her mother died. She went to boarding schools and lived for a while with friends in Tennessee. Summers and vacations she spent with her father and their Negro housekeeper-cook whom she cherished.

She rode horseback with her father, read, sewed, and learned the details of running a house. When she arrived at college age Mr. McCrory did not encourage her to continue her education, but nevertheless she went to a small college in Alabama. Here she joined the YWCA, became prominent in its activities, and volunteered to work as a foreign missionary. Young and idealistic, she wanted to go to India. Going to college had been a long enough journey, however, as far as her father was concerned. He vetoed all plans for India. (Some thirty years later her journey to India in the cause of humanity would be realized by proxy, in the work of her son.)

Julia McCrory had been to Agnes Scott College in Georgia before she went to South Carolina's Winthrop College as YWCA Secretary. She was in her third year of work at this women's school when Weatherford made his Christmas visit. And while he was there, as she later told a friend, she learned the meaning of the old saying, "He swept me off my feet."

On May 27, 1914, they were married in the home of the president of Winthrop College. After a brief honeymoon they returned to Nashville, Tennessee, and to Blue Ridge, North Carolina, and for years to come their home life would be divided between these two places. They built a home in Nashville's residential Belle Meade, on the site of the carriage house of the historic old Belle Meade estate. Thus the Weatherfords lived in the most socially acceptable and affluent section of Nashville. Their egalitarian commitments were not diverted, however, and Weatherford himself continued in his practice of democracy as had his hero, Andrew Jackson, whose handsome home stood on the other side of Nashville.

"Julia," a knowledgeable friend says today, "carried over into her marriage the pattern that had been established with her father of wanting to please. The summers of their marriage were at Blue Ridge. That first summer there, she and Dr. Weatherford shared a cottage with several other people. Building was still going on all over the grounds, conferences were coming and going, starry-eyed students were arriving to work on the staff at Blue Ridge.

"Life there as Dr. Weatherford's bride was a special job in itself. She did not spare herself but gave herself entirely to the exhausting job. It was totally demanding and she gave totally.

"Back in Nashville during the winter she fell into

another pattern with much responsibility but lots of loneliness in the big brick house while Dr. Weatherford traveled and worked harder than three men put together."

During the winter of 1915–16 Mrs. Weatherford was pregnant, and for several months she was quite unwell, a fact she tried to hide from her husband as much as possible. Hovering over both of them was remembrance of what had happened at that previous childbirth. It was a time of happy anticipation tempered by the anxiety of somber recollections.

On June 24, 1916, however, W. D. Weatherford, Jr. was born. Apprehension was banished and only the happiness of parenthood remained. When she came home from the hospital in Asheville with their baby, Mrs. Weatherford was carried down the deep-woods path and across the foot-log of the moss-fringed mountain stream to the new cabin in a secluded corner of the Blue Ridge grounds. This would be the Weatherfords' home for many summers to come.

When Weatherford received a message later that year telling of his mother's death at the age of eighty-nine, the pattern of life seemed almost too neatly carried out. His stout-hearted, strong-minded mother who had been the main influence in his early life was gone. Now there had entered the influence of a wife and child.

Another important member of their family circle came early in their marriage. She was Rosa Lea McKesson, like Mrs. Weatherford a native of Alabama. Rosa Lea McKesson was more than a cook and servant in this household. For twenty-four years she worked for—no, worked with—the Weatherford family, and it was a happy association. And as unforeseen trials of pain and endurance tested the Weatherfords' stamina, the family became more and more dependent on Rosa.

These personal relationships were at the core of Weatherford's private life, but they were also part of those other undertakings, especially the ones at Blue Ridge, that were going forward at full pace.

To Blue Ridge Assembly, between 1912 and 1944, came some 150,000 people. Of these, 3,200 were the special college students Weatherford selected from all over the South to combine an unusual summer of work and scholarship. They helped maintain the grounds and buildings and run the dining room; they took courses of study for which they might receive credit when they returned to their colleges in the fall; and they enjoyed recreation in its truest sense. As for the conferences themselves, they were attended by a wide variety of people. Some sought simple pleasure in mountain climate and scenery; others found a refreshing enlargement of their hitherto provincial horizons; and many discovered relationships which changed their lives.

Every person who came to Blue Ridge also came, more or less directly, under the influence of its creator and administrator, W. D. Weatherford. The place clearly reflected the beliefs animating the man's life. He did not consider the building and administration of Blue Ridge a job in the usual sense of that term. He did not consider his teaching there work in the usual meaning of the word. He once spoke of a "true sense of calling in life," and this sense carried over into this undertaking.

"Work cannot be measured in terms of so many dollars for so many hours of labor," Weatherford said, "but real work can only be measured in terms of what it does to and for people. We dare not spend our energy in doing anything less than making better human beings." This was the philosophy motivating Blue Ridge.

In November, 1919, the first issue of a magazine called *The Blue Ridge Voice* appeared, and its editor, Weatherford, said its purpose would be to "show in some faint measure the sanity and bigness of our program, so that others may come and see that it is good."

Incidentally—or not incidentally at all, but fundamentally and prophetically—the leading article in this first issue was a plea entitled "Law and Order." It called attention to the "menace of mob violence in America" and cited disorders in Washington, Knoxville, Norfolk, Boston, and Chicago, among other places, that were filled with foreboding of events to come. Unfortunately it would take most of the other leaders of the South some forty years to arrive at an outspoken stand for simple "law and order," when that law and order involved the emotion-laden question of race.

If the students chosen to come to Blue Ridge during the summers were the choicest ones the South could offer and if the conferences were numerous and well attended, it followed that teachers and speakers for these sessions must also be persons of high quality. Weatherford believed that people grow by contagion of great personalities. He wanted such a contagion to become epidemic at Blue Ridge.

Outstanding theologians, teachers, business and professional men from all parts of the nation came to speak. Blue Ridge became a stimulating and sometimes controversial place. When, as sometimes happened, neighbors in the mountains or YMCA Board members or some random critic singled out certain ideas or statements from the large assortment of speakers and asked that all such opinions be officially deplored now and forbidden in the future, Weatherford came to the rescue of free speech. He pointed out that it would be as impossible as it was undesirable to try to screen all the ideas that might be discussed during each summer's ferment.

In this connection in October, 1924, he made a statement of some of Blue Ridge's policies and purposes: "We

94

have some two hundred and fifty speakers and leaders on our grounds each summer," he said. "They are all chosen because we believe they have a constructive message. But the freedom of speech among Christian peoples makes it certain that some speaker will say something with which the Blue Ridge Board would not officially agree. In particular where you are dealing with young people it is easy to find some statement which seems hasty or unbaked. But to refuse to let them speak means first that we consider ourselves all-wise as to truth, and, second, it means we bottle up dynamite. It is the nature of dynamite under pressure to explode. Powder never was known to hurt anyone when it was not confined.

"We believe 99 per cent of the things said at Blue Ridge are sound and constructive, forward looking and helpful. The other 1 per cent is purely personal opinion, not the official utterance of Blue Ridge. To avoid this 1 per cent would mean to put a censorship on all expression. This would kill progress and stifle truth at its birth.

"It would be a sad day when such a step was taken. We have confidence that the 99 per cent constructive truth will not be vitiated by the 1 per cent of negative teaching. This is simply the adventure of finding truth and those who will not make the adventure surely will never know the truth."

Dealing, as he hoped, with the totality of life—social, economic, political—as it related to the religious experience, Weatherford and Blue Ridge could not avoid controversy. The situation was not so much that they were ahead of their time as that the society surrounding them was lamentably behind the times. Scientifically, America was only around the corner from the atomic age! In the realm of human relationships it sometimes seemed scarcely out of the stone age.

Blue Ridge was one of the few places in the South at

this time where race relations could be openly discussed. Mention of this topic in most gatherings was greeted with the shocked silence that attended mention of a dread social disease or reminder of some ugly family skeleton-in-the-closet. Not only were race relations discussed, but also Negroes were invited to Blue Ridge to share their ideas. Such exchanges defied the widespread Southern taboo on relationships that did not clearly define the participants as white master and Negro servant. "Nigger" or "boy" or "uncle" were the common forms of address to Negroes of all ages and stations in life. Besides the familiar forms of Jim Crow segregation by law, there were also customs and traditions forbidding such daily conveniences as Negroes' use of elevators in stores or public buildings. Negro customers could not try on the clothes they wanted to purchase in white-owned shops. Public toilets were not for the Negroes' use. Most white Southerners growing up during this time were actually unaware of the many small refinements by which a whole race was locked in humiliation, deprivation, and constant fear. And this callousness, this very lack of awareness on the part of the white dominant majority was one of the most enervating aspects of the South's racial dilemma.

Through years of travel and lecturing and counseling Weatherford had told the college students under his influence, "Look! See!" And as he himself began to see the realities of this racial situation, he could do no less than admonish an even broader audience again to "Look!"

"I had to face the race issue at Blue Ridge," Weatherford has said. "I had to take the responsibility for decisions of policy and courses of action. In such a situation if you stop to take a poll someone is always there to respond in the negative. Then you have to buck an open and avowed opposition, and more often than not you have trouble on your hands. I found that the best thing to do is go ahead! Do what you have to and meet the consequences head-on."

So the eminent scientist Dr. George Washington Carver and the nationally known poet James Weldon Johnson and the president of Tuskegee Institute, Dr. Robert Russa Moton, and other Negroes came to Blue Ridge as honored speakers. Dr. Carver made a profound impression on all who heard him. ("The humblest man I've ever known," a Brown University official would recall thirty years later.) Mr. Johnson told Weatherford, as he was departing after several days at Blue Ridge, that he had never been more hospitably treated anywhere. As for Dr. Moton, he and Weatherford had become good friends and would work together on several fronts during the years to come.

Dr. Mordecai Johnson, president of Howard University in Washington, told a student conference at Blue Ridge in June, 1926: "If I had a thousand young white men in the South who would treat every Negro that they came in contact with with the radical love of Jesus Christ, and a thousand young black men who could accept the challenge of those consecrated lives and treat every white man and white woman with the same spirit, those two thousand men would create a revolutionary atmosphere in a single generation that would challenge the thought of the world on the Negro question."

Another year Dr. Ashby Jones, white Atlanta Baptist minister and internationally respected spokesman of brotherhood, stated his conviction "that the efficiency of the Christian religion never found a more insistent challenge than in the relationship of the races in the South."

He wondered if his listeners dared to consider that "the Negro is as completely within the power of the white man today as in the days of slavery. From the Potomac to the Rio Grande there is not a single political office which he can hold. He can serve on no political committee nor enter into conference in any political caucus. The great bulk of the property, and the management of great commercial enterprises, is in the hands of the whites. Nearly all of the great institutions of civilization, schools, hospitals, libraries, art treasures, and facilities for recreation, are in the control of the whites.

"Here is the most dangerous position in which any people can ever be placed. It is the position of absolute power without responsibility. The moral strain is greater than that of slavery. It is not wholesome for any group of people to be given such power over any other group, without any restraining sense of responsibility. The Negro is taxed without representation. He is governed by laws in the making of which he has no voice. He is summoned before judges in whose election he has had no word. The result, as was inevitable, has been that, as a race, he has not received justice. He has been commercially exploited. He has been forced to live under the most unsanitary conditions. He has had poor educational and cultural opportunities, and his chances for the development of his highest possibilities have been limited."

With such radical talk as this going on at Blue Ridge the wonder is that the institution survived. Sometimes there were anonymous threats when it became publicly known in advance that a Negro speaker would appear on the program. One summer a Negro secretary attended the assembly of all the YMCA student secretaries of America, and a disgruntled white man in the neighborhood made his disapproval of this integration known. Weatherford had already made it a *fait accompli,* however.

A few weeks later all those at Blue Ridge were awakened one night by the smell of smoke and the sight of fire. The laundry building behind Lee Hall was ablaze. In the midnight confusion about all that could be done was contain the fire and keep it from spreading.

This was accomplished, and only the small laundry house was destroyed. Weatherford believed that the vindictive white man had set the building afire as a protest and warning. Weatherford refused to be warned, however.

He later said, in another context, something that applied equally well to this situation: "I told those men they'd better not get me in a corner. I had learned that when I was a boy growing up in Texas: you corner a coon in water and he'll fight back. I'll fight back too."

Problems of racial intolerance arose almost daily. There were small situations that seem exquisitely trivial today, but then they could have ruined a good man's career for the rest of his life. After all, it had not been too long since President Theodore Roosevelt's audacity in entertaining Booker T. Washington at the White House had rocked the government to its foundations.

One day a photographer snapped a picture of an outstanding liberal professor from a Southern university as he stood talking with three Negro friends. At Blue Ridge this might seem a perfectly sane and normal situation; but such a scene, suggesting any equal social exchange between the races, could, in the hands of a demagogue, destroy the future careers of all involved, both white and Negro. Weatherford had to intervene and secure the photograph and negative of this picture, so innocuous and yet so explosive.

For students who came from the cotton and turpentine country of the Deep South, where the name "Black Belt" counties denoted not only fertile earth and masses of Negroes but a mental attitude as well, the experience of hearing such strange new ideas was catalytic. One woman said, years later, "I went to Blue Ridge from Mississippi. I didn't know Mississippi had a race problem! During one of the first discussions I spoke up, 'In the section where I live the people are three to one Negro and everybody is happy. We don't have any problems.' Everyone in the room just looked at me. It wasn't long before I learned how ignorant I was of the very place where I lived. Blue Ridge set me free in a way most people would find difficult to understand. It was a place of *seeing*, of vision."

Another young man went to Blue Ridge both before and after World War I, and the experience proved good training for the battlefield. His Blue Ridge introduction to respect for all people followed him into his career as an ambulance driver with the French Army. He told Weatherford later, "While carrying black men whose bodies were shattered by high explosives or ripped by shrapnel, it came to me that I could never again look on these men as inferior. If they were willing to die for those values which we all consider precious, who was I to try to say that they were not to be treated as equals because of their color?"

Later, after working in prisoner-of-war camps in Europe and with the British army of occupation in the Middle East, this man returned to the United States, graduated from the Yale Divinity School, and became Secretary of the YMCA at the University of Virginia. Then he returned to Blue Ridge, half fearful that he would find it marking time in the realm of interracial ideas. To his surprise and gratification he met several new Negro leaders of the South and found himself among some of the young white men who were becoming the advance guard of a racial and political liberalism in the region. He wrote Weatherford, "It was your vision, enthusiasm and courage which created at Blue Ridge a seedbed from which grew and developed leadership which has spread all over the South, to other parts of the country, and to different parts of the world."

The questions of racial justice and understanding which were wrestled with at Blue Ridge were only slightly more controversial than some of the other subjects to which speakers addressed themselves. Politics, for instance, was scrutinized.

Whenever it was possible to praise one particular political leader for some courageous moral stand, either a speaker at Blue Ridge or an editorial in the *Voice* often called public attention to the action. Governor Albert H. Roberts of Tennessee was commended for his forthright and forceful policy of law enforcement at all levels. The governor was encouraging prosecution of lynch parties and maintaining resistance to mob violence at a time when the Ku Klux Klan was in one of its periods of resurgent despotism. Exposure and continuous denunciation of such extralegal secret organizations remained important. The Klan, during these years following World War I, boldly expanded its scope of influence. KKK floggings and lynchings continued in the rural Deep South but were supplemented by efforts to gain power in the border regions and in burgeoning industrial communities in the North. Success in seizing such power was made possible because of large migrations to the North by both races, which brought about the displacement of some whites by Negroes in jobs and housing. Tensions fostered by such direct competition provided a ready atmosphere for growth of the Klan, and during the 1920's the KKK became almost as much of a force in Indiana, Illinois, Michigan, and several other Northern states, as it was in the South. Vigilantism, Klan style, became an ugly part of the national scene; political careers were wrecked; intimidation was a ready whip used against many classes of people, from migratory field hands to foremen in the factories to governors in their executive mansions.

During these years, quite a stir was aroused in the halls of Blue Ridge when one of the most brilliant and respected lecturers of years past (and years to come) stood before the group and said at one point in his discussion of politics and religion, "What is the attitude of the church today on mob lawlessness? I am more eager for my pastor to stand in opposition to the Ku Klux Klan than to be sound on the Virgin Birth."

There were other ideas that aroused attention and kindled sparks. Dr. Samuel C. Mitchell, a Virginia professor, asked a student one day, "Sir, how do you spell 'politics'?"

The young man answered by giving out the letters: "p–o–l–i–t–i–c–s."

To which Dr. Mitchell replied, "You are wrong, sir. It is spelled o–i–l!"

One Blue Ridge student said, "Dr. Weatherford and his staff had a marvelous way of relating the coal scuttle to the universe."

If the South had been held by the dead clutch of traditionalism in racial concerns, it had been gripped to a degree almost as stifling by traditionalism in industrial relations. One of the chief topics for discussion at the first Southern Sociological Congress in which Weatherford had participated had been child labor. It was inevitable, of course, that Weatherford's agenda at this conference center should include consideration of religion applied to industry.

As he told those who wanted to know about Blue Ridge and its purposes at that time, "We are trying to find the attitude of Jesus toward human life. This cuts deep into modern industrial and business life. Who would dispute that our modern social order is not yet ideal? Is it not worth while to try to find Jesus' attitude toward human life and then constructively apply that attitude in our relation to others in business, in manufacturing, in race relations, everywhere?"

Another Blue Ridge stalwart had put it, "He is Lord of all or else He is not Lord at all."

One of the earliest conferences held at Blue Ridge dealt with industry and religious precepts, and by July, 1922, when the third Southern Industrial Conference on Human Relations in Industry was held, a record attendance of over four hundred and fifty could be reported. Thirty-three company presidents, vice-presidents, general managers, secretaries, and treasurers were present, along with forty-five superintendents and one hundred and fourteen foremen. They represented textile, lumber, furniture, iron and steel, coal, paper and pulp, printing, and proprietary medicinal industries. Presidents of some of the best-known manufacturing companies in the South were on the conference committee: H. R. Fitzgerald of Dan River Cotton Mills in Virginia; A. H. Bahnson of Arista Cotton Mills in North Carolina; James R. McWane of McWane Pipe & Fitting Company in Alabama, among others.

The keynote talk at that meeting, made by Charles R. Towson of New York, must have struck a responsive chord in Weatherford. The interesting point is that, with a few alterations of emphasis, the four main points of Towson's address had long been and still are part of Weatherford's plea for closer attention to the possibilities of poverty or plenty inherent in the cybernetic revolution today.

"Education has not kept step with industrial development," Towson said. "The churches' progress has not kept pace with the development of industry. Industry has outstripped our other institutions, and we must recognize this."

He went on to point out that "the biggest factor in industry is not machinery, material or money, but the human factor. And the biggest thing in the human factor is not body or mind, but spirit. Believing this will lead to a new estimate of values concerning four things."

His four points included reverence for the sacredness

of personality, necessity for personal contact and man-to-man confrontations in a spirit of mutual interests, recognition of need for self-expression on the part of industrial laborers, and, finally, renewal of a sense of service on the part of all who work.

Some of the influential leaders who participated in these conferences became the forerunners of a new and enlightened management group. There were, however, other industrialists in the South who disapproved of even the public airing of subjects which they considered their private preserve. They resented the temerity of ministers, professors, newspapermen, and those they generally termed "do-gooders" who would presume to discuss industrial matters.

A wealthy and powerful North Carolina tycoon became especially irate over Blue Ridge's presumption. He leveled a sharp attack on this conference center which "infested" the hills of his own state. Who could tell when its dangerous practice of exchanging ideas might contaminate the whole region? His attack produced no initial results, however, and the administrator of Blue Ridge showed no disposition to change his programs.

The manufacturer then tried another approach. He chose a member of Weatherford's Blue Ridge Board and threatened this man (a dealer in stocks and bonds) with loss of clientele if Weatherford's activities in discussions of the industrial relations and racial fields were not curtailed. The beleagured board member went to Weatherford and told him of the ultimatum he had received.

Weatherford replied, "I'm running Blue Ridge. Tell that man to run his plant. If that's not a big enough job for him, let him go ahead and shoot at me. We'll see what kind of game he brings down."

When his bluff was called, Weatherford's opponent backed down on his threat. He continued carping at the

Blue Ridge program, but his objections had lost their force in the showdown.

The staunchest supporter Weatherford found in his industrial relations work was John J. Eagan, President of the American Cast Iron Pipe Company in Birmingham, Alabama. Eagan, too, was a man with a mission, and his life and Weatherford's became closely linked. Eagan eventually added another dimension of influence and interest to Weatherford's life, just as Weatherford would add a new and continuing dimension of depth to the huge and competitive industry in which Eagan was successfully engaged throughout his life.

In August, 1923, Eagan spoke at Blue Ridge on subjects that were not usually given public attention by executives of heavy industry. What he had to say provided a sharp picture of the industrial worker. It embodied the essence of Blue Ridge enlightenment on the subject.

With administrative abruptness Eagan launched into his subject. "I would call you to face your responsibility as leaders of men. Stockholders, executives, foremen, whichever you may be, the true function of industry today is making men.

"How well have we succeeded and how well are we succeeding? Statistics show that at least one-third, possibly one-half of the families of wage earners employed in manufacturing and mining earn in the course of the year less than enough to support them in anything like a comfortable and decent condition. Do you men know the slums of your community? And do you know the ones who live there? Do you know how many of your own working men live there?

"In these slums in Atlanta, Birmingham, Chattanooga, or wherever they may exist, you will not only find the down and out, the misfit, but many wage earners. On the other hand, you may find men broken by industry. Do you know that the number of men killed by industry in America averages twenty-five thousand a year, and that seven hundred thousand are injured in one way or another every year, so as to be incapacitated for work for four weeks and over?

"Three per cent of our population owns sixty per cent of its wealth. Sixty-six and two-thirds per cent of the population own five per cent of its wealth. An average of ten million people in our country are living in poverty. It is not going to help us to try to make our task, the making of men, seem easier than it is. Corporations are organized to make money, and we are all working for corporations. Now how are we, in a system organized and designed for the express purpose of making money, to make men?"

This was no dedicated labor leader, no wild-eyed young radical dreamer speaking. This was a multimillionaire businessman who had been successful at making both pipe and men. And he gave his formula: first he named the necessity of providing a living wage.

"Tell me that a corporation cannot afford to pay a living wage, and I will tell you that corporation ought to go out of business. In your own corporation, how many of your men are living in places you would not live in? From four to eight times as many babies die in the poorer sections, where many of your workmen live because they are unable to live elsewhere, than in the well-to-do sections.

"Another item—reasonable hours and working conditions. In this country an average of two and one-half million people are in bread lines and hunting jobs. And while these men are trying to support the family that may be starving, other men are working twelve hours a day seven days in the week!"

The last two items he brought to his listeners' attention were profit sharing and employee representation. Both of these were fairly unique ideas at this time. But American Cast Iron Pipe Company, with Eagan as its leader, had tried both profit sharing with its laborers and consultation with its workers on matters of policy and conditions and wages, and had made them succeed. When he called upon industrialists at Blue Ridge to follow these steps in making men as well as money, he spoke from experience and success.

Weatherford took quiet satisfaction in Eagan's leadership in this great untested field that would soon have so many tests put to it. Within a few years Weatherford himself would have reason to know much more about the "Eagan Plan" and ACIPCO than he did at the time Eagan made this talk at Blue Ridge.

These topics—religion, race, politics, and industry— were by no means the whole substance of Blue Ridge, but they indicate the general atmosphere of courage and freedom in which all aspects of life were examined. And there were almost no other places where such sustained discussions were going on in the South during those decades.

A variety of outstanding men returned to Blue Ridge year after year. If, as Weatherford believed, character is caught, not taught, he wanted to expose his conference participants and particularly his working students to those with the germs of ideas and those with characters strong enough to be "catching."

John R. Mott came upon numerous occasions to Blue Ridge, and those who encountered his inspired messages were not likely to forget the experience. As Eugene Barnett, who himself became an international leader of men, said, "I first met Mr. Mott (as he was then) and saw him in action in a southern Student Conference which I attended as an undergraduate in the Blue Ridge Mountains of North Carolina. The impression he made on me was much the same as that on the Montreal columnist who once dubbed him, 'the Day of Judgment in breeches.'

"What a master of assemblies Mott was! He held vast audiences in thrall and generated among them influences which reached to the ends of the earth. At the same time he gave incredible attention to the smallest details, leaving nothing in the appointments and arrangements to chance. He liked to quote his friend, Theodore Roosevelt, who said, 'Detail makes perfection and perfection is no detail.' He elected to take the qualities, and not a few of the methods, which created tycoons and towering political leaders in the America of his time, and dedicate them to the furtherance of Christianity."

Old associates of Weatherford's, especially O. E. Brown, Dean of the Vanderbilt School of Religion, and Edwin Mims, head of that same university's Department of English, were at Blue Ridge almost every summer. Several of the faculty members from the YMCA Graduate School, which Weatherford founded in Nashville in 1919, also came to the mountains to teach during the summer months. The man who taught in both places for perhaps the longest period of time was John Louis Kesler. Kesler had taught science at Baylor University, but during the period of divisive debate between science and religion he had been dismissed from the faculty. Subsequently he had gone to Europe, where he had become interested in the study of psychology.

At the Graduate School and at Blue Ridge he lectured on the psychology of religion. One of his students later recalled: "His lectures were above anything I had known before. Listening to them was as though I were supposed to be on a plane when I was actually on the ground watching the plane overhead. But I came to love as well as admire Dr. Kesler. At Blue Ridge he used to say that the mountains were his though he owned not a foot of land. Those who owned the libraries were not those who bought the books, but those who read and understood the books."

(In 1945, when he had become professor emeritus of religious education at Vanderbilt, Dr. Kesler made a gift of fifty thousand dollars to the university to establish a circulating library for rural ministers. Vanderbilt's chancellor, Oliver C. Carmichael, called it "the most generous gift, all things considered, of which I have any knowledge." The project of such a library for rural ministers had been initiated under Kesler with the backing of the Carnegie Fund, and after his gift, the university's Board of Trust added fifty thousand dollars and called it the John Louis Kesler Circulating Library for Rural Ministers. This was the sort of practical idealism Weatherford sought out and inspired, and Kesler was the sort of man Weatherford stood by during periods of storm.)

Dr. William J. Hutchins, father of three sons who would become distinguished educators, had assumed the presidency of Berea College in 1920 and had become a trusted associate of Weatherford's. He was a frequent Blue Ridge speaker. So, too, was Will Alexander, Director of the Commission on Interracial Cooperation in Atlanta. For a time the Alexanders had a cottage not far from the Weatherfords. Mrs. Alexander and their three sons—along with the Robert B. Elcazers and their two sons and daughter, who also lived in a nearby cottage—became good friends of the Weatherfords and of Willis, Jr.

Robert B. Eleazer carried forth much of the research, writing, and publicity for the Interracial Commission, and over the years he became one of Weatherford's most devoted friends. Eleazer was a gentle, scholarly man whose rather delicate physique sometimes misled strangers into assuming that he was not forceful. Nothing could have been farther from the truth, for this man conducted personal investigations of the KKK and a secret organization called the Black Shirts at a time when physical danger was very real. He was publicly and privately threatened on several occasions. Through his writings—distributed by the Interracial Commission to schools, newspapers, and organizations throughout the country—he revealed many neglected aspects of Negro-white relations in the South.

Personal compatibility between Mrs. Eleazer and Julia Weatherford cemented the friendship, and as Willis grew up an only child, he found companionship in the Eleazer and Alexander children.

Many other able and outstanding men helped create that stimulation and meditation which co-existed at Blue Ridge. One of those on the Blue Ridge staff when it opened in 1912, who helped direct its course for more than a quarter-century, was Edward S. King. For thirty-six years King was YMCA Secretary at North Carolina State College in Raleigh, and the quality of his contribution at Blue Ridge may be ascertained from an editorial which appeared in the Raleigh *News and Observer* at the time of his death.

"He was a Quaker, and he was a quiet man. And he was agreeably stubborn in his support of what his Quaker conscience told him he must do, but his quietness and affability could never be confused with timidity or unwillingness to fight if it came to that point. Nobody, least of all Ed King, ever knew how many meals he bought for hungry people, or how many train and bus tickets he bought for those stranded away from home. Nobody knew how many discouraged students he persuaded to stay in college, or how many students he helped climb from pitfalls into which they had fallen. Nobody knew those things except those who were helped." And nobody except King himself could have said how much "Uncle Willis," as he called Weatherford, helped shape and sustain the influence of his work.

Dr. Samuel Chiles Mitchell, President of the University of South Carolina, before and after which he was a professor at the University of Richmond, returned to the assembly for twenty summers. Grey hair, neatly trimmed mustache and goatee, and bright twinkling eyes gave him an elegant appearance. His animated style of speaking, free of all notes, his ready humor and wide knowledge of history, his sometimes iconoclastic views whetted the intellectual appetites of eager students. He was one of their most popular teachers. And he, too, liked what he found at Blue Ridge.

One year Dr. Mitchell was asked by Columbia University to teach history at that institution's summer school. He wrote to Weatherford, asking for his reaction to this invitation. Knowing that Columbia could pay more than double the salary Blue Ridge offered, Weatherford replied that he would be deeply sorry to lose Dr. Mitchell from his faculty, but under the circumstances Mitchell should go to Columbia. The prompt reply from Richmond said, "I will be at Blue Ridge this summer."

Other notable Southerners who came included the North Carolina Poteats, a pair of progressive and dynamic brothers, and their sons. W. L. Poteat was head of the biology department at Wake Forest College and later its president, and E. M. Poteat was professor of religion and later president of Furman College in South Carolina. McNeill Poteat, son of E. M. and an outstanding Baptist minister, delivered his famous lectures, "Coming To Terms With the Universe," at Blue Ridge. He contended that religious men must be fitting into, not fighting, the scientific truths of the universe. The Poteat family was remarkable. Forward-looking and fearless, they flooded many a rostrum and pulpit in the South with fresh air and light.

Political leaders of the region spoke at Blue Ridge: Governor Thomas Walter Bickett and Governor Robert B. Glenn of North Carolina, Governor A. H. Roberts of Tennessee, Governor C. H. Brough of Arkansas. William Jennings Bryan of national fame also took the assembly platform on several occasions. Other notables came from many professions and corners of the South: Smith Richardson of Greensboro, North Carolina, later founder of the Richardson Foundation; President H. A. Morgan of the University of Tennessee; Dr. J. H. Dillard of Tulane; Dr. E. C. Dargan from the Baptist Theological Seminary at Louisville; Bishop Theodore Bratton of the Episcopal Church of Mississippi; and Bishop C. B. Wilmer of the University of the South at Sewanee, Tennessee. Clarence Poe, Raleigh, North Carolina, editor of the *Progressive Farmer* magazine, brought wit and wisdom to his insights on a new rural South. Dr. John Gandy, President of Petersburg, Virginia, State College for Negroes, and Dr. Monroe Work from Tuskegee Institute made fellow Southerners aware of some of the neglected problems of Negro life. Bishop Robert Jones of New Orleans addressed Blue Ridge assemblies, as did Mrs. Mary McLeod Bethune of Florida, an institution in her own right.

Although they were strongly Southern in spirit, purpose, and content, Blue Ridge assemblies and classes were not narrowly provincial. Many of the finest speakers and teachers returned year after year from other sections of the country. Among these were Dr. H. H. Horne of New York University and Dean Charles Brown of Yale University; Robert Speer, one of the nationally renowned lecturers of the period who participated in Blue Ridge programs for twenty-two successive summers; Dr. Henry Sloan Coffin of Union Theological Seminary and Dr. Harry Emerson Fosdick, pastor of New York's Riverside Church; and Dr. J. Campbell White.

E. Stanley Jones held the first of his famous "Ashrams" at Blue Ridge. Dr. E. T. Colton, an expert on the vast, puzzling, and increasingly powerful country of Russia, spoke at Blue Ridge, as did Sherwood Eddy, seeker after new enrichments of the social environment.

Even Ernest Thompson Seton, then famous throughout America as the author of *Wild Animals I Have Known,* came to Blue Ridge as a representative of the Woodcraft League. He worked with boys and built several simple cabins with native materials. He and his League wished to combat an illness they deplored: "Thingitis." David E. Lilienthal, Director of the Tennessee Valley Authority, spoke during the 1930's.

Of the thousands who visited Blue Ridge, however, those uppermost in Weatherford's concerns and affections were always the students. In 1923 he wrote, "Of all the groups that come to Blue Ridge each summer, the Summer Staff of 'P.W.G.'s and P.W.B.'s' are unique. They remain for three months under the inspiration of the conferences and the mountains, the fellowship of God and man."

Because he did feel that the natural surroundings were as important as any lectures men could devise, he and Mrs. Weatherford—who had developed into a true Highlander despite her Lowland girlhood—led many hikes each season. Some were short and meditative. Some were long and strenuous, pushing students unaccustomed to the heights until they sometimes felt their chests would burst or their legs would collapse if they took one more step. At this point Dr. Weatherford might appear by their side, take the pack and add it to his load, and quietly encourage them to go the last lap to the top of the mountain. There were sunrise hikes and overnight camps, and the climax each year was a two-day journey to Mt. Mitchell. This pinnacle of the Black range was

113

the highest peak east of the Mississippi, and it stood twenty miles distant from Lee Hall and the big old rocking chairs on the comfortable veranda. A night on its slopes might be filled with rain or moonlight, wind or stillness, but the view from its summit seemed to encompass the world.

At Mrs. Weatherford's request Dr. Kesler organized wild flower hikes, too. Her interest in making plants and flowers more familiar to the students also enlarged their appreciation of conservation. Dr. Weatherford adamantly opposed anyone's picking a leaf or flower for selfish pleasure; every plant should be left in the rich Blue Ridge woods for others who would come later to enjoy.

In 1956 a United States senator who had been a Blue Ridge student wrote Weatherford: "I recall so clearly the admonition that you gave to young men: 'Pray without ceasing and shave every morning!'" Weatherford might climb the heights, but he insisted on keeping his feet on the ground.

Those students who worked in the kitchen soon discovered that Weatherford was no less interested in them as dishwashers than as students. He would walk through dining room, kitchen, halls, workrooms, blue eyes searching out each corner like the roving lens of a flash camera, registering each detail; and he was quick with commendation for what was well done, even quicker with condemnation for anything half-done, shoddily sloughed aside.

Mrs. Weatherford's influence at Blue Ridge was important. Fortunately she had taught physical education at college, and on the plantation where she was reared she had frequently ridden horseback with her father and had become familiar with the out-of-doors. Her husband wanted her to share in every aspect of life at Blue Ridge: mountaintop hikes, overnight camping, adventures with wet and cold, inadequate blankets or short rations or frights-in-the-night that are an indispensable part of every camper's log of memories.

She joined in many of the athletics at the assembly, too, and the students were impressed by this tall, handsome couple who seemed to combine in their persons and in their marriage an enviable balance of physical fitness, intellectual vigor, and spiritual radiance. When Mrs. Weatherford invited the young people to special functions at her cottage or fixed a favorite dessert for one of the hikes or made some other appropriate little personal gesture, it remained memorable because she discharged her duties with a quiet sense of taste and style.

Only the fullest effort and the highest achievement on the part of his students could satisfy Weatherford. His own appearance—immaculate high white collar, vest, gold Phi Beta Kappa key, carefully polished glasses which sparkled no less than his quick glance—denied even the possibility of sloth. Its example influenced those around him.

He could not tolerate haphazardness. The epigram that punctuality is the courtesy of kings might have been written of him. Two P.W.B.'s learned this on their first arrival at Blue Ridge. A couple of Alabama boys, having missed their train connection in Birmingham, reached Blue Ridge several hours later than they were expected. They thought a few hours would make no difference to anyone. When they entered Weatherford's office he immediately asked why they were late. One of them explained the train situation. Weatherford reminded them that the telegraph offices were still open and telephones were still functioning. It was their duty to inform anyone expecting them if they were delayed en route.

More than punctuality was involved in this incident. It indicated Weatherford's watchfulness over those in his trust. He cared about those two boys, and he was troubled when they did not appear on time. Such concern communicated itself to young people.

One of the more important examples of this concern and the confidence it could generate is still clear in the memory of Dr. Frank Graham. On the morning of June 28, 1913, a group of Southern student secretaries of the YMCA had gathered at the railway station in Black Mountain, North Carolina, waiting for the train and special pullman car that would take them, under the supervision of Weatherford, to Estes Park, Colorado, and the conference for student secretaries from all parts of the United States. Also at the station but waiting for a train from the opposite direction, which would take him back home to Charlotte after his stay at Blue Ridge, was Frank Graham, then a student secretary at the University of North Carolina.

Weatherford spotted Graham at the station and went to tell him of his regret that the boy was not going to the national gathering at Estes Park. Graham replied that he wished he could go, but that he simply did not have the money for the trip. Weatherford said without hesitation, "I'll lend you the amount for the round-trip ticket." They went to a bank across the street, and within a few minutes Graham had received enough money for the journey. Where Graham was to sleep and how he was to eat were problems to be faced after he got on the train. Weatherford helped him get a job waiting on tables at Estes Park, and this paid for a cot in one of the student tents and three meals a day.

In Colorado, Weatherford entered with such zest into the classes, discussions, games, mountain climbing to Long's Peak, and anything else that came along that his boys were ashamed to show anything less than equal fervor. When time came for the annual baseball game, Weatherford's determination to have his South succeed

116

surged to the forefront. In this game the four regions—North, West, East and South—and their sub-regions, played against each other until one was acclaimed champion. Final play-off that year was between the South and the Midwest. Weatherford wanted the South to excel here as he wanted it to excel in so many other ways, and he fired the spirits of his team.

Frank Graham was in the outfield on that game, and during the last inning when the score was tied and the Midwest had men on second and third, a fellow named Tracy Jones hit the ball high and hard. It seemed that the South's chances were doomed. But Graham, running toward the fence with his eye trained on that ball as it came through the high clear Colorado air, put every ounce of effort and form he knew into that catch—and then the throw to home plate—and the honor of the South was saved! Whenever old friends remembered that great moment in later years, Graham reminded himself that there were two people who had won the game that day. One of them was a man who could stir others to go beyond even their own highest expectations.

One professor who taught for a summer session at Blue Ridge told Weatherford frankly that he thought he drove his students too hard. Every week night was designated for study, and the heavy reading schedule imposed on the students required that the library be left open each night until ten o'clock. But Weatherford replied to the critical teacher by showing him the lists of names of those students who had asked to return for two, three, four years—and the long waiting list of those who wanted to come to Blue Ridge.

Why would young people want to come back year after year to the stern discipline and hard work of this assembly in the North Carolina hills? One answer must be that it filled needs deeper than those which could be satisfied by vacations that were frequently over-long and without purpose. A man from Georgia once said, "Weatherford's definition of sin as the deliberate choosing of less than the best made real sense to me at a time when I was searching for meaning in religion."

Many young people were searching for such meanings. Another, who became a minister in New York City, recalled taking the bus from Oxford, Mississippi, to Blue Ridge. "It was more than a bus trip. It was a trip to another world, a mental and spiritual world of which I had an inkling but which was to be unfolded to me in three short months. I have never gotten over that bus trip nor the overwhelming feelings which came over me that late, rainy Sunday afternoon when I arrived and stood on the porch of Lee Hall looking over the valley."

Solomon Levy, a six-foot-two veteran of World War I, participated in conferences with Weatherford and told his friends, "Well, I think I've found here a kind of religion I can believe in."

One young man who came to Blue Ridge had grown up on a plantation adjoining one owned by the uncle of Ross Barnett, who would become the intransigent segregationist governor of Mississippi during critical years of the late 1950's and early '60's. How important was the influence of Weatherford and his institution in creating the difference between these two Mississippi boys who grew up as neighbors and then took such different paths into the twentieth century? This man, who is now a professor at a Mississippi college, says, "Nothing in my experience compared to the summers of work at Blue Ridge Assembly.

"Dr. Weatherford knew each one of us by name, and we felt free to take any personal problem to him. No one did as much work as Dr. Weatherford; no one played as hard. He required the same of all his students. Someone must have convinced him early in life that one cannot do all he can do unless he undertakes to do more than he can do."

This particular fellow speaks from experience of "taking any personal problem" to Weatherford. While attending both the Graduate School at Nashville and Blue Ridge, he fell in love with one of the girls also at Blue Ridge. Penniless, they went to Dr. Weatherford to ask what they should do.

Weatherford plunged both hands into his pockets, drew them forth, and said, "Here are my car keys. Here is some money. Go to Asheville, apply for your health certificate and marriage license, and arrange for a minister to perform the ceremony."

After they were married Weatherford continued to let this young man earn his college expenses by working as head janitor ("We gave it the high-flown title of Maintenance Engineer") at the Graduate School during the winter, and rolling and keeping up eight tennis courts at Blue Ridge ("We called it Grounds Supervisor").

Agnes Highsmith came as a P.W.G. to Blue Ridge and the experience changed the course of her life. She was a tall, intense girl with curly dark hair, vivacious and eager. Her father was a judge in Georgia, and when she first arrived at Blue Ridge she had just finished her freshman year at Wesleyan College in Macon, Georgia.

"When we send one girl to Blue Ridge," Agnes' faculty adviser had told her, "we are doing it for everyone at the school. It changes a whole class."

Agnes Highsmith's mother believed that her daughter was going to an exclusive sort of resort-assembly, and when she came to visit Agnes that summer and found her carrying heavy trays as she waited on tables, Mrs. Highsmith was dismayed. Agnes' enthusiasm for this somewhat new experience of work soon quieted all of the older woman's fears, however. And each summer for years to come, as a student at Wesleyan, at the University of Georgia, at Columbia University, and finally at Yale, she returned to Blue Ridge.

"Dr. Weatherford always started with you where you were," Agnes Highsmith says. "He didn't say, 'You're prejudiced,' or 'You're backward.' He simply showed you the reasonableness of treating other human beings justly, courteously, and you moved on from there. I studied at Columbia and I received a degree from Yale, but I never had an educational experience equal to Blue Ridge.

"When I was at Yale, anxious friends would keep asking me how I was getting along in my studies. And I'd say, 'Fine. I passed Dr. Weatherford's course in the Philosophy of Religion, and that's harder than any Yale course I've encountered.'

"Another thing: when I went to Yale, I went to the student employment office, and when the woman there asked me what work I would do, I said, 'Oh, I'm from Dr. Weatherford's. I'll do anything. The dignity of labor, you know!' We'd learned our lessons well at Blue Ridge!"

Another student who had been at Blue Ridge with Agnes Highsmith, for whom Weatherford had also obtained a scholarship at the Yale Divinity School, was David Braswell. There was no little irony in the fact that one of the few Negro students then at Yale consistently chose to sit with one or both of these Southerners when they were in the dining room. It seemed to be *that* student's opinion that liberated Southerners were less self-conscious with Negroes than most Northerners. "We didn't talk about being integrated at Blue Ridge," Agnes Highsmith says; "we just were."

In addition, Dr. Weatherford accorded girls the same intellectual respect he paid boys. "When I got to Yale one

of the professors assigned the seats in his class alpha-
betically, but he had three girls in the class stand against
the wall while this was being done. Then he had us seat
ourselves at the back of the room. When I wrote my first
essay for him, I said, 'At Blue Ridge I was treated as a
human being. Here I'm treated as a girl.' "

Weatherford said to his students: "Blue Ridge is life
—working, studying, playing, worshipping—not just
preparation for life." He wanted them to know that any
excellence—good food, a well-made campfire, thorough
study, meditation on a hill-top, friendship with others—
was part of that plenteousness necessary to a rich life.

Julia Weatherford and Rosa Lea McKesson made
delectable individual pecan pies for the students to take
on their mountain climbs. Sometimes in the evening a
group would sit on the steps of the Weatherford cottage
and listen to a nearby whippoorwill. These activities
and lectures on applied religion in industry and politics;
romance and swimming and hard-won games of tennis,
handball, baseball; the gold curtains of the library and
the icy water of the morning showers: all these were
part of the experience of Blue Ridge.

One day long after she had been a P.W.G., one of
Weatherford's former students brought her small son to
see the place where she had spent several memorable
summers of her youth. They stood on the wide steps
leading up to the broad veranda framed by its tall
white columns and together contemplated the breathtaking view in the distance, beyond the gently rolling
woodland and the avenue of pines leading away from
Lee Hall.

And as they looked the little boy turned to her suddenly and asked, "Mother, when did God and Dr. Weatherford make all these mountains?"

She had to smile, remembering those times when
Weatherford's fatherly concern and patriarchal author-

ity had instilled a similar awe in some of the young people here.

In February, 1927, Weatherford wrote to his Blue Ridge friends: "I have a little boy ten years old. My work takes me each summer to Blue Ridge, North Carolina, where I have a summer cabin in the mountains. I have a big spring just above that cabin which supplies water at a temperature of fifty-three degrees when it comes into the house. When my little boy was just five years old he began taking cold showers in this fifty-three-degree water. One morning when we stepped into the shower he looked up at me and said, 'Daddy, it takes a real man to do this, doesn't it?' My friends, it takes a real man to be a religious leader, and no man dare undertake so momentous a task unless he has the very highest motives and unless he secures the best training that it is possible to secure."

For thirty-two years, from 1912 to 1944, Weatherford undertook the momentous task of a religious leader and educator at a place called Blue Ridge Assembly where he hoped to inspire and train an indigenous effective leadership for the whole South. When he finally resigned, it was because the load of fund-raising, administration, and teaching had become too heavy to carry along with the other concerns and work to which he was also addressing himself.

It has been said that in his life nearly everybody encounters one great teacher, a person who profoundly influences his life and thought. For hundreds of people who importantly influenced the South, Weatherford was such a teacher. Blue Ridge and the Graduate School in Nashville provided him the means by which he could reach these individuals. Weatherford and many of his students were yeast in the healthy ferment of a growing, changing South.

When he was asked not long ago what major obstacle

he encountered in making Blue Ridge a success, he did not mention the threats of racial bigots or the opposition of religious fanatics or the attacks of political demagogues.

"The biggest obstacle," he said, "was indifference."

Today, confronted with the even more urgent necessity of finding men who will see our regional, national, and world problems in their wholeness, in their interdependence, Weatherford again meets the old enemy, indifference. The indifference of individuals trapped in their own private problems and small vision; of bureaucracies smothered under the weight of their own machinery; of institutions confined to past realities that are no longer realistic and techniques that are no longer effective. Above all, he confronts the indifference born of a poverty of faith—too little faith in man, no faith at all in God.

The biggest problem Blue Ridge faced was indifference, but by the sheer force of his personality, physical vigor, and determination of will, Weatherford made it live and flourish and influence thousands of lives scattered around the world today.

11

William Goodell Frost, President of Berea College in Kentucky, came to Blue Ridge for a visit in 1915. He stayed a week. At the end of his visit he had a long conversation with Weatherford which he concluded with an invitation. "You are doing the same thing here that we are at Berea: combining work and study. You must come on the Board of Trustees of Berea."

Weatherford's affinity for this college that served mountain boys and girls was natural. The institution had been born in conviction of the dignity of each human being and his right to education, and it had had a fight all the way. In the early 1850's an influential Kentucky landowner, Cassius Clay, had persuaded an outspoken young antislavery minister, John G. Fee in northern Kentucky, to come to southern Madison County and make his home. In 1855 a one-room school was built on the ridge where Clay had given Fee ten acres for a homestead. The site, the board, and the labor had all been contributed by local men who wanted a school for their community.

One gift for the new little schoolhouse came from New York philanthropist Gerrit Smith. In his later years Fee liked to repeat the story of that donation. When he told Gerrit Smith of the work that he was about to establish in Berea, Smith replied, "It's impossible. They will not allow you to establish an antislavery church or school in Kentucky." "Well," said Fee, "I am going to try." And Gerrit Smith told him, "Here is fifty dollars to help you try."

Such a beginning was something Weatherford could appreciate. Indeed, Fee and Weatherford would have made good companions in many ways. The former named his newly established school Berea, after that town mentioned in the Bible where men were open-minded. And although, with the approach of civil war and during the conflict itself, the mob spirit blazed high in Kentucky and Fee was nearly hanged while his comrades were beaten with rods and his wife kept fearful vigils through the nights, he never retreated from his racial stand. Years after the war Fee's daughter exclaimed, "Why, we supposed everybody had mobs."

In 1869 Henry Fairchild came as president of Berea, and he went through the days of the rise of the Ku Klux Klan by "tactics of acquaintance." Knowing the Kentuckian's reputation for hospitality, he asked the names of those men in the community who were most hostile to Berea. Then he would drive to see them, taking his wife along. He usually managed to arrive at meal time, and the mountain people always invited strangers in their midst to take a meal. Such acquaintance made it difficult to attack a man, and although there were occasionally wild ridings and shootings into homes, klansmen never visited Berea in force.

William G. Frost, a professor of Greek at Oberlin College, came to Berea as president in 1892. The school had been interracial since 1866 and soon after his arrival a nearby county official told him: "I can tell a Berea 'nigger' the minute he comes into my office—he is neither cringing nor obtrusive."

Frost immediately began putting into action his proclamation that "Berea is an engine of universal civilization. It must carry on many forms of education at once —teaching the people how to get a living, and how to live."

Like Weatherford, Frost wanted to know first-hand the circumstances of the people around him. His curiosity took him and his wife into the back country, where he persuaded parents to send their children to school. Often he felt that he was "riding into the last century" as he became acquainted with spinning, weaving, fodder-pulling, herb-digging. He was intrigued with the place-names which seemed to have come straight from the Anglo-Saxon imagination and local incidents. He made long lists of these names: Bear Wallow, Rabbit Hash, Whynot, Lonesome, Viper, Scrabble, Pine Knot, Knuckles, Stanaround, Troublesome Creek. It was just such places that Weatherford would be visiting, in Kentucky and elsewhere, in behalf of Berea many years after Frost's journeys.

Frost was sometimes overwhelmed by the noonday "snacks" offered at the mountain homes he visited, and he described them to friends in other sections of the country: "There is hot cornbread, buttermilk, string beans, pork, preserves and stack pies everywhere, and commonly early potatoes, tomatoes, onions, endless fried chicken and blackberries; occasionally honey and pickles . . . after which the President of Berea commonly asked a chance to lie down for an hour."

Mountain and Negro dialects met and mingled on Berea's campus. Frost worked to erase all barriers between people. By the turn of the century, when there appeared a small flood of books inciting hate and fear of Negroes, Frost took the sales agency for one of the most vicious, entitled *The Negro a Beast*. Thus he prevented its circulation in the state and secured a quantity

of the books at agents' prices. These he used to dis-
tribute among his friends in other regions and alert them
to the rising tide of renewed prejudice. Frost believed,
as did others, that this revival of persecution was a cal-
culated condition brought about by politicians who
feared that Theodore Roosevelt was becoming too
popular in the South. Such opinions seemed justified
when, in 1904, Kentucky passed a segregation law aimed
directly at Berea, the only integrated college in the state
at that time. (A similar law in Tennessee affected Mary-
ville College, a Presbyterian institution near Knoxville.)

For five years after this law was passed President
Frost devoted the largest part of his time and energy
to the Negro cause. By 1909 he seems to have felt that
he must choose between his fight to reinstate Negro
students at Berea and his struggle to increase and improve mountain education. Later critics might contend
that he deserted both the Negro's and, to some extent,
Berea's cause. He, however, felt that his college stood
before the public as the representative school for mountain people as Hampton and Tuskegee represented
institutions for Negroes. It was a cruel choice and one
that could only prolong the South's major problem, post-
pone its moment of truth.

As Frost turned to those white hill-country students
who needed Berea so desperately, he also had to find
donors to finance the buildings and salaries Berea required. He wanted to develop a work program that
would enable students without money to make their
way through school, and he also aimed at adapting
Berea's men and resources to the solution of problems
in the mountain area of eight states.

"He knew," one friend has written, "that the mountain
problems were too great for one generation to solve, but
he could never forget the illiteracy that made life dull,
the isolation that bred feuds, the ignorance that made

life harder than it need have been, and the poor teaching that handicapped every mountain child. Although he sometimes waxed sentimental over the log cabins and the spinning wheel, more often he was grim at the thought of the bareness of the mountain man's inner life."

While he was still considering whether to accept the presidency of Berea, Frost made careful inquiry concerning the school's facilities for self-supporting students. The president of Oberlin had assured him that manual labor experiments always fail, but Frost was not convinced of this. On the day he accepted leadership of Berea, as Dr. Elisabeth S. Peck has written, Frost "persuaded the trustees to pass another resolution, one which has been of great importance to self-supporting students ever since that time: that tuition was to be free. Although a small incidental fee was retained to cover the cost of such services as heating and caring for classrooms, the charge to cover the expense of actual teaching was removed, and from 1892 to the present Berea College has had no tuition fee."

To make such a system possible, philanthropists, educators, leaders in all other parts of the country had to be made aware of Berea's existence. By 1915 this had been accomplished to such an extent that both Chief Justice of the United States Supreme Court Charles Evans Hughes and President Woodrow Wilson made speeches in Washington in support of Berea College.

No aspect of Berea's history or program won wider attention than the success of its student work program. Some of the vocational courses introduced early in Frost's presidency, such as carpentry, agriculture, and cooking, were taught in part by the apprenticeship method. Others—printing and bricklaying, for example —were taught entirely by practical work without regularly scheduled classes.

The range of work at Berea was wide, from the bakery to the library, from the dairy barn to the woodworking shop, but its purpose was not to earn income only; along with the classroom it was an educational tool. As Weatherford looked over Berea and became familiar with its plan, he felt at home with its philosophy and practices. He understood the student who wrote after her graduation from this school, "My labor experiences helped me grow toward maturity. The people who know me are not my roommates, nor my teachers or classmates, but the people with whom and for whom I worked."

Ninety per cent of Berea's students came from the two hundred and thirty Southern Appalachian counties stretching fom West Virginia to northern Alabama.

When Frost suggested to Weatherford that the latter should join Berea's Board of Trustees, the acceptance was not surprising. With their philosophies of egalitarianism, education, and labor coinciding so happily, and with the almost apostolic concern each had for the mountain region, it would be difficult to see how they could have avoided their relationship.

In 1916 Weatherford joined the Berea College Board. For half a century he would give Berea support and would help shape, through the college, understanding and fulfillment of the entire Southern Appalachians. For thirty-five years he would be vice-chairman of the Board, and during the majority of those years he would be chairman of the Education Policy Committee. But even more important than these services of leadership were the energy and prayer, threat and plea, gasoline and shoe leather that he would expend in getting as many worthy students as possible from the isolated mountains to Berea.

This move in 1916 into the official family of Berea was a culmination of interests and a forerunner of projects that claimed more and more of Weatherford's attention. He was becoming increasingly involved with the mountain people, especially the youth.

He was moving, too, toward establishment of two agencies that would be as prophetic and influential as any similar institutions in the South at that time. One was the Commission on Interracial Cooperation in Atlanta; the other was the YMCA Graduate School at Nashville. Before they were begun, however, there were the challenges of a world war to be met.

12

"Ignorance," Weatherford once wrote, "is not an excuse. It is a crime."

Of the many poverties this man has spent his life combating, none has seemed to him more important to conquer than ignorance. His definition of the word was far-reaching. It included illiteracy which came from lack of schoolroom experience and also the illiteracy which stemmed from lack of common sense, ineptitude in finding practical means to achieve a goal. It included the uneducated who scorned delving deeply into books or ideas and also those who were untutored in the needs and aspirations of the human spirit. One of the most deplorable types of ignorance, in Weatherford's log, was a man's lack of knowledge about his work, how to do the most efficient and effective job of which he was capable, no matter how large or small the undertaking.

When World War I came and the YMCA accepted extensive work with the armed forces, Weatherford felt that many of the YMCA workers were not prepared for the strenuous demands of this new calling. Perhaps he feared that the generally conservative background of the YMCA would hinder fullest imaginative use of this opportunity.

Writing his history of the YMCA in North America, C. Howard Hopkins discussed the YMCA's relationship to the public affairs of the nineteenth century. "Like the churches from which they sprang," he noted, "they hardly considered 'the world' their province, assuming that its ills were due to the machinations of evil men under the Devil's control and that conversion to the Christian faith offered the only possibility of social reform or genuine improvement. . . . Its leadership was so completely identified with the cult of materialistic success that any suggestion that its goals might be questioned would have been regarded as 'communism' . . . . Whatever the social liberalism of the secretaryship may have come to be, the social gospel had small effect upon the leadership of the local Y.M.C.A."

This may have continued to be true for many state and city associations, but the student movement of the association was for the most part different. Certainly its Southern International Student Secretary was different. In fact, Weatherford was totally out of accord and patience with interminable debating societies and patent-medicine approaches to social problems. He prodded the YMCA to probe deeper and work harder toward understanding and alleviating problems.

With the eruption of World War I an obvious opportunity for enlarged influence presented itself. Subsequent investigations reported: "The Young Men's Christian Association had laid upon it an enormous task by virtue of its acceptance by the Government as an agency of moral welfare in the Army and Navy. Not only was the task enormous, it was also most delicate and difficult, requiring the Association on the one hand to preserve its loyalty to its own character and its relation to the churches, and on the other hand to observe every propriety and obligation as an authorized agency of the Government."

Soon after the beginning of the war Weatherford talked with John R. Mott at the conference center in Northfield. He pointed out that most of the army camps would be located in the South because the weather there would permit longer training periods, and he asked Mott why the YMCA had not done something about helping strengthen men spiritually in these camps.

"We don't have the leaders," Mott replied.

"Then you haven't tried to get them," Weatherford said. "Let me send one hundred telegrams, signing your name, and we'll find leaders."

"Go ahead," came the answer.

Those telegrams, written by Weatherford over Mott's name, produced results. Men of ability and training were found to work in the Southern army camps.

In addition, a war work school was established at Blue Ridge where secretaries for overseas camps could be trained. Weatherford soon realized the size of the job Mott had handed him. The War Workers' Training School involved assembling, in the period of a few weeks, a staff; preparing to house and feed 150 men at each school of a month's duration; gathering a faculty of fifteen or twenty of the ablest professors in the region; setting up a course of instruction that would fit these men to see the needs of soldiers and answer them, recognizing that those needs would be many and varied. All this had to be done in less than a month.

Preparations were made and the training got under way. Weatherford's job then included the task of keeping Blue Ridge running smoothly, holding regular meetings of the faculty, interviewing students, visiting New York once during each school period so that he could report on the work to Mott, visiting Atlanta during each term so that he could counsel with Dr. Will Alexander and S. A. Ackley, who were holding similar schools there, and—to be sure he stayed active—teaching the entire school for an hour each day when he was at Blue Ridge.

A faculty of professors from Duke and Vanderbilt and other Southern universities was assembled for this war work school. Weatherford ran his usual tight ship. Eight schools of three weeks each provided intensive training to eight hundred and twelve men who came from throughout the country. And every man who came to Blue Ridge was personally interviewed by Weatherford, who wanted to be sure that each one understood the purpose of the school and why he was there.

The eighth intensive session of the school was drawing to a close when the Armistice was signed.

Peace had come, but a few thoughtful Southerners realized that the racial problems facing the South might make it a tormented and bloody domestic truce. Foremost among these far-sighted men were Weatherford and Will W. Alexander. "Dr. Will," as the latter became known throughout the nation, was, like Weatherford, a Westerner born (Missouri) of transplanted mountain Southerners (North Carolina and Tennessee). Also like Weatherford, he had been trained in the Methodist ministry, graduated from Vanderbilt, and—until his war work—had been a minister in Nashville.

Firm friendship between the two men had begun during an exchange when Alexander was filling the pulpit of Belmont Methodist Church in Nashville where Weatherford was a frequent member of the congregation and his wife taught a class of college-age girls. The incident revealed much about the character of both men.

During the winter of 1914–15 Nashville, Tennessee, was gripped by economic depression. War in Europe had curtailed the cotton market just when the South was harvesting the largest cotton crop it had ever produced. Price of this staple plummeted to five-and-a-half cents a pound. Even with the new mechanized Progress that was dangling such bright hopes of prosperity over the region, the South's economy was still tied to cotton—and five-cent cotton spelled disaster. Numerous factories in Nashville closed that winter, and a new urban word came into use throughout the city: unemployment. Empty cars crowded railroad yards; posters urged citizens to "Buy a Bale" of cotton and help destitute farmers; leaders of the city thought briefly of opening soup kitchens, then decided Nashville did not want the publicity that would accompany such a move. In the poorer sections, suffering was acute. Alexander had been out among some of these people, and on a Sunday morning in December, as he stood in his pulpit and addressed the nice comfortable middle-class people who made up his congregation, he found himself telling about the desperate plight of those who lived just across town.

This was unusual, but it provoked an even more startling occurrence. As he finished his description of conditions he had seen and the people he had found, someone in the congregation spoke out. "What do you want us to do about it?"

It was precisely this question that Alexander dreaded, had not dared ask himself. He did not know what to do. But Weatherford had put it squarely to him, lifting hunger, cold, and need from the realm of discussion into the arena of action. A collection was taken and turned over to Alexander that morning, further financial aid came from other sources, and in a short while Alexander had a community program under way that alleviated existing conditions and provided some firm steps for future progress. Perhaps most important, W. D. Weatherford's question brought Alexander for the first time to the role he would play so constructively for the rest of his life—that of one of the important social architects of our times.

Alexander left the ministry to join in the war work.

He never returned to the pulpit. Experience with Southern soldiers had brought him face to face with the South's two great problems: poverty and race.

"You saw it," he said, "as you looked at the army. The illiterate whites were the product of poverty, and the Negroes were the product of poverty plus discrimination."

He saw that the evils were inextricably linked and that until Southerners began to deal realistically and imaginatively and justly with their racial and economic dilemma they could never attain their best. Alexander had received one of the Weatherford-Mott telegrams. After his work with soldiers was finished, he, along with Weatherford and a few others, saw that the racial conflict was just beginning. He would devote his life to reconciliation between races and regions in this country.

Eventually he became one of the creators of Atlanta and Dillard Universities in Georgia and Louisiana. Under President Franklin D. Roosevelt he was administrator of the Farm Security Program. An innovator of measures which accelerated Negro progress on many fronts, director of some of the more creative philanthropic funds in the country, Alexander was destined to become one of the most influential Southerners working for racial progress. At the close of World War I he stood at the threshold of his career.

Among the faculty of the war work school held at Blue Ridge in November, 1918, was L. Wilbur Messer, an outstanding YMCA leader whose work in Chicago had gained a wide reputation.

On the day after the Armistice, Weatherford engaged Messer in a long conversation during which he pointed out that problems were sure to arise as the country began to receive its soldiers returning from overseas. Weatherford emphasized that those Negroes, especially, who had been welcomed into white homes in Europe, would not be willing to resume the subservient, second-class role they had accepted before the war. Furthermore, they should not accept it.

Messer understood Weatherford's message and its urgency. They called in Will Alexander and discussed the situation at greater length. Alexander was already deeply disturbed, too, over the paradox that gripped America.

"It seemed to me," he said, "that we had enjoyed a period of freedom and had suddenly realized that freedom was dangerous, and we retreated from it. The South had always mistrusted things from the outside, particularly ideas, and now this mistrust turned to fear. We had struggled to make the world safe for democracy and now we realized that democracy was dangerous, and we became confused."

Dimensions of the retreat and confusion may be summed up by a statistic of that first postwar year. It was a season of "almost unmitigated horror and tension," as one Negro leader described it. More than seventy Negroes were lynched. As they were beaten, mutilated, shot or burned to death, several of the victims still wore the uniform of the United States Army.

Weatherford, Alexander, and Messer met with a group of thoughtful white men in Atlanta in January, 1919. They wrestled with the race problem for the better part of a week, discussing ways to diminish the fear and hysteria that seemed to be growing among both Negroes and whites, seeking some means by which both peace and justice could be won.

Alexander kept reminding these men how well the South had behaved, for the most part, during the war. Then, for the first time, white men had come in contact with Negro leaders in their communities. Until then there had been far closer communication between white and Negro bootleggers than between white and Negro ministers or educators or civic leaders. As they pondered this situation it seemed that the most practical course open now was to go back into these communities and get the people who had worked together on war bond drives or other wartime activities to work together now for peacetime purposes.

"Here was something," Alexander said, "that didn't affect the world but did affect their own communities, and racial violence threatened the peace of those communities."

The idea was to assemble, as quickly as possible, a staff of two men—one Negro and one white—for each Southern state. They would go to the towns and cities where tensions were worst, and they would seek to bring people of both races together to find ways to meet the local situation. Judged the way in which any social innovation must be judged, that is, in the context of its times, this was a bold and creative idea. Inherent in it, as its subsequent development would demonstrate, was capacity for growth and adaptation to shifting times and different places. This was an important aspect of its success.

To carry out this plan, however, funds were necessary. Initial efforts soon made it evident that money for any racial—not to mention interracial—cause would be hard to come by. Weatherford suggested that this was work in which the YMCA should be interested; he, Alexander, and Messer went to New York. There they presented their concerns and their plans to John R. Mott, Cleveland H. Dodge, and Cyrus H. McCormick. These men approved of the idea and granted an initial appropriation of seventy-five thousand dollars from funds left in the treasury of the War Work Council.

Thus, in 1919, the Commission on Interracial Cooperation, or the Interracial Commission, as it came to be called, was created. The field workers went out into the counties of the South, and by July they could report conferences in 452 counties. In churches, courthouses, banks, private homes, a few men, white and Negro, would talk about the problems that faced them and agree on some first steps toward meeting those problems. The field workers weren't always skilled or successful conference leaders; the results of these first tentative meetings were not always clear-cut and affirmative; but something new was happening in the South, and here and there apprehensions were being lifted, improvements were being won. And that was no small victory.

One difficulty which faced the undertaking was the poverty of leadership in the South. Weatherford returned from New York to Blue Ridge and began a series of "schools," or conferences. Before he was finished he had held ten in all, attended by some 1,216 white leaders. These included Southern lawyers, doctors, teachers, businessmen, and religious workers. For ten days each group stayed at Blue Ridge and worked toward making some constructive plans for the communities in which they lived.

At the same time, Will Alexander in Atlanta was conducting eight schools for some 509 Negro leaders.

The genius of the plan this Interracial Commission had devised was two-fold. First, it was grass-roots; it involved local citizens in local situations and problems and encouraged them to seek their own solutions. Second, it brought both races into consideration of racial problems.

"Our plan," Will Alexander later said, "was an effort to substitute reason for force. It was unique in that it was an effort to deal with the problem not by resolution, or general proclamation, but at the county level through groups of citizens well known in their localities and to each other. We were further trying a new method in appealing jointly to white and colored citizens to work together in solving the problem. Heretofore, the Southern custom had been for white folks to decide what they wanted and tell the Negroes to do it, with the ever-present assumption that the white man would use force if necessary."

For almost a quarter of a century the Interracial Commission was influential in the South. In the early 1940's it evolved into the widely respected Southern Regional Council, whose present headquarters are still in Atlanta.

Weatherford was one of the moving spirits behind the founding of the Commission and its early work. Some of those with whom he labored were among his closest friends and outstanding Southern leaders. In this undertaking and in numerous others their paths crossed and crisscrossed as each sought, in his own way, to make the South a land of plenty for all its people. The picture of Weatherford's South and his life and work would not be complete without acquaintance with a few of these men who aided in organization and direction of the Interracial Commission.

There was James Hardy Dillard, Virginian, former Dean at Tulane University (where Weatherford had first known him), a member of its Board of Trustees, also a member of the influential General Education Board founded by John D. Rockefeller and supported by his millions. Dillard was also director of the Jeanes and Slater Funds which had made significant contributions to Negro education.

Another member was John J. Eagan, the industrialist who has already been mentioned, and will be again.

Meredith Ashby Jones, an important participant in the group, was the son of a former chaplain to Robert E. Lee, and he was pastor of an influential Baptist church in Atlanta. It was said that his eloquent statements of the case for democracy had inspired thousands in their war effort. He had expected the war to "strengthen democracy in the South," he said. When war did not seem to achieve this goal, he was willing to go to work to make peace (and a more perfect justice) "strengthen democracy in the South."

S. A. Ackley, Regional Secretary of the YMCA, and R. H. King, a native Southerner, brought a background of years of area work into their interracial contributions. King had served on the War Work Council, too.

Plato Durham, a North Carolina graduate of Trinity (now Duke University) and Yale and Oxford, was on the faculty of Georgia's Emory University. He enjoyed the special respect of many Negro co-workers and became a particularly effective member of the group which was formed.

Among the Negro leaders who joined this interracial venture was Robert R. Moton of Tuskegee, already mentioned as a good friend of Weatherford's and a lecturer at Blue Ridge. He was the very tall, very black, very wise son of slaves and the direct descendant of African chieftains. He was determined to further the cause of Negro education in the South.

Also there were Robert Elijah Jones, North Carolinian and editor of the *Southwestern Christian Advocate* in New Orleans, the only Negro bishop in the M. E. Church; and John Hope, one of the truly outstanding Negro leaders in the nation, at that time president of the institution later known as Morehouse College. During the war Hope had served in France as a special YMCA secretary, an experience which depressed him and at the same time impressed him with the need for Americans to make some effort toward meeting a racial situation that was rapidly becoming unbearable. His attitude was wavering between deep cynicism and pale hope at the time he joined the Interracial Commission. Association with the white men in this group helped reaffirm his confidence that progress might be possible.

Two other active participants were John M. Gandy, Mississippi-born president of Petersburg Institute in

Virginia, who had worked with Negro soldiers in various army camps during the war, and Isaac Fisher, publisher of the *Fisk University News* at Fisk University in Nashville.

One of the first local situations the Interracial Commission participated in while it was yet in process of formation involved a vote by the city of Atlanta on a proposed bond issue to build more schools. Negroes opposed the bond issue, and white city officials did not know why—until the Interracial Commission undertook to talk with Negro citizens. Then they discovered that this minority feared—with justification, surely, since there was not even a Negro high school in Atlanta at the time—that little or none of the money from sale of these bonds would go for Negro schools.

Through the commission's work a promise was secured from the city administrators that if the bond issue were passed a Negro high school would be built. When another vote was taken, Negro support brought about passage of the bond issue. And this one example of tangible results, of what might be done with some communication established between the races, of what was possible through cooperation, assured the Commission's survival.

John J. Eagan was selected as the first chairman of the Commission on Interracial Cooperation. Will Alexander was its executive director then and for twenty-odd subsequent years. W. D. Weatherford remained one of its directors as long as it was in existence, then he became a member of the Southern Regional Council which succeeded it, and finally in 1965 he was elected a Life Fellow of the Council.

In putting his moral imagination, social concern, and capacity for work into the Commission on Interracial Cooperation and by helping secure the funds which were its life blood, Weatherford had made another contribution toward abolition of one type of poverty (in fact, several types of poverty as they intertwined).

Early in its existence the Commission had to return to the War Work Council chest of the YMCA for more funds. Appropriations of some $400,000 were received. Eventually, money from the large foundations would assure the Commission's existence.

The real strength of this interracial movement lay in its local committees. At one time there were as many as eight hundred groups scattered throughout the South. These, as Weatherford once said, "were the essential genius of our Interracial Commission. Local committees brought the best members of both races face to face and made them conscious of the friction points that existed and provided them means by which to lessen the friction."

The goals of the Commission were first, improvement of interracial attitudes out of which unfavorable conditions grew, and second, correction of injustices and betterment of conditions affecting Negroes. More specifically, the aims and accomplishments of the Commission included: legal aid in cases where Negroes were being exploited or intimidated; improvement of police forces; more accurate and affirmative news accounts of Negro life and work; better civic facilities such as sewers, street paving, water, lighting, and playgrounds; increased social agencies and welfare care; and an all-out struggle against peonage and the ultimate degradation of lynching.

The Commission was thus able to improve the physical plight of Negroes who had too often been helpless to help themselves and the spiritual plight of whites who permitted or were blind to such neglect.

Gunnar Myrdal, in his definitive study, *An American Dilemma*, summed up the achievement of the men who had founded and worked for the Commission on Interracial Cooperation, and he concluded: "One of the most important accomplishments of the Commission—which has a far-reaching cumulative effect—is to have rendered interracial work socially respectable in the conservative South."

As Weatherford had begun his work in the colleges for the larger purpose of making religion intellectually respectable in a time of trial and doubt and change, so he also worked with other like-minded men to make interracial work and cooperation socially respectable in a time of increasing upheaval.

Those of us living in the South of the mid-1960's who have had either close or distant experience of the useless waste and blight and death attendant on the racial progress of recent years cannot help but wonder at how different current history might have been if Weatherford's voice, and the labor and foresight of those working for the same goals he envisioned, had been heeded and accepted by large numbers of Southerners. Perhaps the wonder is that they achieved as much as they did, considering the glacial pace at which social change often seems to come, barring revolution itself. But Weatherford's way was always evolution—through the force of example, through the process of education. Always he returned to education as the most powerful weapon against poverty of body, mind, or spirit.

13

One of Weatherford's most ambitious educational adventures began in 1919. In that same year when he participated in pioneering the Commission on Interracial Cooperation, he founded the Southern YMCA College, which soon became known as the YMCA Graduate School, in Nashville, Tennessee.

This was a rather remarkable institution. Any latter-day assessment of its goals and achievements must conclude that its academic reputation for excellence far exceeded its size in numbers; its intellectual influence outlived its physical existence by several generations. Like Blue Ridge, it was, as Emerson has said of institutions, the lengthened shadow of one man. And that was its strength and its weakness, its glory and its downfall.

When Weatherford began work on establishing the Graduate School, he resigned as International Student Secretary of the YMCA. He left behind him YMCA buildings scattered over many campuses from one end of the South to the other, buildings constructed with funds he had secured.

But from those seventeen years as a student secretary Weatherford bequeathed more than buildings to the South and the nation: young people and professors and educational leaders whose spiritual life had become more firmly rooted, not through platitudes and dogmas, but through their own thought and study and uses of philosophy, science, literature, and logic. Weatherford had brought the fire of his own moral faith and intellectual honesty and physical vigor to the podiums and gymnasiums and sanctuaries of campuses across the country, and he had kindled sparks. Now, however, he was ready to found an educational institution whose chief purpose would be to help alleviate a poverty of local leadership in his region.

Until this time there had been two YMCA colleges in the country—one in Springfield, Massachusetts, and the other, George Williams, in Chicago.

Perhaps it would be interesting to note here that just as Dr. John R. Mott had been one of the most influential forces in Weatherford's life, so Weatherford had exerted an influence on the older leader, too. During the earliest days of their association, Mott had taken rather lightly Weatherford's continuous, almost nagging, advocacy of thorough training for all religious leaders, laymen or ministers, and especially for student secretaries of the YMCA. Mott believed, for the most part, that youth, buoyancy, and enthusiasm were essentially sufficient, while Weatherford argued that firmer qualities were necessary—knowledge of comparative religion, literature, and philosophy. On several occasions Weatherford felt that he was somewhat audacious to dispute with Mott on this or any other point, but Weatherford simply could not bring himself to be quiet and through acquiescence desert his convictions in a matter he considered so important. His insistence seemed to be having some influence when, in 1914, Mott laid the cornerstone of the YMCA college in Chicago and took that occasion to emphasize the need in the organization for well-qualified and learned leaders. He said those leaders should be prophets, and he hoped they would be apostles. Such an advance in Mott's public statements had brought him into even closer alliance with Weatherford, and their subsequent undertaking to train World War I leaders had merely underscored the validity of their view.

If there were already two YMCA colleges in existence in 1919, why was another one necessary? A serious handicap to the nation-wide effectiveness of both Springfield and the Chicago school, as Hopkins, the YMCA historian, points out, "was reflected year after year in the small number of students attending them from the South. There were at least three reasons for this: both colleges' programs were geared to the demands of work in the larger cities, whereas much Association work in the southern states was carried on in smaller places. Distance played a large part in the problem faced by the needs of southern Associations. Most formidable was the fact that YMCA's in the North paid larger salaries than did those in the South, so that the best talent from the South often failed to return after obtaining an education at one of the Association colleges."

The success of the war work training schools which Weatherford had suggested and which had been carried on during World War I had convinced some of the YMCA leaders that a permanent training school should be located in the South. The state secretaries of the Southern YMCA proposed Weatherford for the presidency of such a school and urged that he should take this office.

Weatherford hesitated. Although he was the moving force behind establishment of the school, he was well aware of the distance which separated his thinking from that of many of the men who were urging him to assume its leadership. They, too, knew that he was much more liberal than they were, but they also knew that if anyone could succeed in such an enormous venture it would be W. D. Weatherford.

Finally, Will Alexander went to see Mrs. Weatherford to discuss the situation with her. He tried to enlist her help in persuading Weatherford to become head of the Southern college. As Alexander left he said with more vehemence than his mild manner usually betrayed, "There ought to be a law in the Y.M.C.A. to compel a man so well prepared for such work to accept it!"

At a meeting of the state secretaries and leaders of the region, Weatherford finally faced the issue squarely. He told these men that they knew he was liberal. They need not expect him, if he assumed this office, to take over someone else's narrow theological doctrines or social gospel inhibitions. "At this school we are going to face up to issues and look at all sides of questions, whether they're controversial or not," he told them.

Knowing that a few of these same petitioners had made the life of one progressive educational leader in the South a "pure hell," Weatherford abruptly turned to a man in the group and called him by name. "You've been criticizing me for years, trying to tear down my work in the colleges. What are you going to do if I take this office as president of the college?"

Caught off guard, the man stammered that he would support Weatherford.

Then Weatherford turned to another of his critics of the past. "What about you?" he asked. "Can I count on you?"

And the second man assured him of his support. He would help Weatherford raise funds for the school, and he would back him in matters of academic excellence.

So it went around the room. The majority of these men had long been Weatherford's friends, of course, and now they sincerely proposed to lend him all the assistance they could muster if he would accept this important new job.

Thus he became president of the Southern YMCA College. He soon found that this job also entailed being chief fund-raiser, administrator, faculty dean, student counselor, and, above all, the key professor. But Weatherford had a dream for this school. John R. Mott once characterized Weatherford's idea for his college as "prophetic." Hopkins concluded that it "was the most challenging and possessed of the greatest potentialities of the several professional educational ventures attempted by the Associations."

Hopkins describes the venture thus: "It was Weatherford's purpose to set this newest YMCA college at the heart of some great educational center. That locus was found at Nashville, with Vanderbilt University, Peabody College for Teachers, and Scarritt College for Christian Workers all willing to co-operate. Under the interrelated curricula developed, students were required to take half their work in the institution in which they were originally matriculated, but were free to choose the remainder in the other colleges. Thus, Weatherford's physical education majors might study their human anatomy under medical instructors at Vanderbilt. The proximity of the four co-operating schools was such as to make the interchange of classes easy, a resource tragically denied to Chicago YMCA College students by the mile of tangled traffic separating that institution from the University.

"The Southern College—the school soon became 'the YMCA Graduate School'—also had available the services of several hundred professors—specialists in all lines. 'With a faculty of a dozen men, the college could be run and courses could be as varied as would have been possible with half a hundred professors,' wrote

Weatherford in retrospect, and 'credit taken in one institution was applicable to degrees in all of the co-operating institutions. The arrangement was well-nigh perfect in its advantages to the YMCA.' Another resource was one of the greatest libraries in the South, the negotiations for which were facilitated by Weatherford's good offices."

Weatherford's own informal statement on his aims at the college said, "I would rather train five men a year to think and act for themselves than to train one hundred to acquire a mere smattering of standardized information. It is not our function at Southern College to teach men what to think but to teach them how to think."

His own persistence in securing an education, his constant reading and study through the years in a wide variety of disciplines, and his many conferences and exchanges with leading educators had prepared him for the work of leading this college.

The catalogue issued by the YMCA Graduate School stated: "It [the college] goes on the assumption that while technique alone is absolutely essential to a successful secretary, technique alone will not make him a success. The school expects its graduates to do more than carry on in an approved way the approved activities of an Association. It expects them to be community leaders, to have that trained mind and vision which not only sees but comprehends community needs, and it expects them to possess the intelligence required to organize community forces to meet such needs."

This was indeed avant-garde. The largest religious denominations of the region were already experiencing a serious and growing schism between their educated and uneducated ministry, between those who preached and those who opposed the so-called social gospel. Many ministers were poorly trained, and the majority of their congregations felt that "a call" to preach was far more important than any sustained study or preparation for this momentous task. A man who proposed to be a doctor and keep the human body healthy should have long and rigorous instruction before he began to practice; anyone who proposed to sustain the health of the human spirit could set up shop with only his sincerity as his qualification.

Weatherford admitted that the man who stood, at this time, for stiff training of religious leaders had a hard battle to fight. But he must have kept in mind the image that he had invoked before of that coon cornered in water, for he fought on. Insight into the history and scope of religion coupled with the inspiration of a creative experience of God: when would community religious leaders be raised up who combined such qualities?

The student body of the Graduate School was a small but select group. "I just love to see a boy or girl who has a lot of drive," Weatherford once said. "You know nothing can hit him hard enough to make him stay down: the kind who'll always get up and go."

The new YMCA Graduate School building was located on Hillsboro Road in Nashville, and the school also occupied Wesley Hall on the Vanderbilt campus. The faculty varied in size from ten to a dozen professors, and the students were convinced that their teachers could not be equaled in any similar institution. Many of the men were well-known scholars in their fields who welcomed an opportunity to teach in an open atmosphere where they could stimulate their students to free and frank discussion and exchange of ideas. Formal classes at the school were characterized by a sense of purpose coupled with respect for sound scholarship.

In addition, classes at Vanderbilt, Peabody, and Scarritt provided a wide range of choice in subject matter. Weatherford also took students on visits to Tuskegee Institute in Alabama and to nearby Fisk University, just across town in Nashville. Few if any other Southern schools were making such exchanges at that time. The accepted pattern was for white and Negro colleges within blocks of each other, in the same city, to be completely unaware of the other's existence. Although each institution might be poor, especially in comparison with its Eastern counterparts, and hard put to secure outside cultural enrichment, there was no cooperation in securing lecturers, concerts, or other such programs. And certainly there was no cooperative effort to understand mutual community or regional needs and problems. For some of the students at the Graduate School, Weatherford's act of introducing them to the campus and people of these great Southern Negro colleges was their most memorable educational experience.

Courses in religion, philosophy, psychology, sociology, and physical education were stressed at the Graduate School. Sometimes the various disciplines were enlisted in one project so that a problem could be viewed from many angles and the possibility of finding permanent solutions be enhanced. For instance, in 1932 *A Survey of the Negro Boy in Nashville, Tennessee* was published by the Association Press. This survey had been made under the general direction of Weatherford with eight research specialists carrying forward a detailed examination into the daily life of the Negro boy in Nashville. In his introduction to the published volume Weatherford made it clear that for his purposes research was of value insofar as it provided direction and impetus for subsequent action. He said: "When the social agencies of a community speak of serving the boys of that community, one usually needs to ask whether they mean all the boys, or just the white boys. As an organization, the Young Men's Christian Association has officially declared in favor of 'full participation in the Association Program without discrimination as to race or color,' but we know that is a goal to work toward—not a fact of achievement. In order that the social agencies of Nashville might know fully the needs of Negro boys, the Y.M.C.A. Graduate School undertook a careful survey of a cross-section of the Negro boy life of the city. We have hoped that such a study might be of value to other cities wishing to study the needs of their Negro boys; and, in particular, we have hoped that it would stimulate many Y.M.C.A.'s to undertake constructive work for and with these boys."

The statistical findings of this study were eloquent testimony to the impoverished life the majority of Negro boys led. A sentence in the chapter on juvenile delinquency might have summarized the general findings: "The Negro boy in Nashville has been treated in such a manner as not to minimize his delinquency but to aggravate it."

In addition to formal classroom work and outside study, Weatherford also taught his students by the force of his example and attitudes. One day when a member of the Graduate School was asked to go to Fisk University and speak, he came to Weatherford with a problem.

"How should I talk to them?" the man asked.

"To whom?" Weatherford asked.

"To them—the Negro students."

Weatherford's eyebrows shot up. "Why, talk the way you do to everyone."

During these years of the Graduate School, Weatherford was running Blue Ridge in the summers, of course, and the work of these two institutions became closely intertwined. Many of the same students went to both places, following the more formal academic patterns at Nashville during the winter, enjoying the intensive courses of study during the summer in the tonic atmosphere of Blue Ridge. One couple might exemplify some of the others. Paul Derring, of Virginia, had been blind since a night in February, 1906, when he was twelve years old and had been shot in the face by a careless playmate. In the darkness from which there was no escape, he had heard a doctor say, "You'll never see again, but don't feel that failure lies ahead. Your best chance is to get an education."

With his sister's help Paul Derring went through William and Mary College and earned a Phi Beta Kappa key as well as a diploma. He married a librarian, Katherine Cook, and together they enrolled at Weatherford's Graduate School and at Vanderbilt. Derring had come under Weatherford's influence during one of the latter's visits to the William and Mary campus. In Nashville and in North Carolina that influence and friendship was intensified, and when Paul Derring received his M.A. degree he went to the Virginia Polytechnic Institute in Blacksburg, Virginia, as YMCA secretary. Later he was made director of religious activities, and he stayed at this school, inspiring generations of students with his personal courage and lively wit, until his retirement at the age of seventy.

Several members of the Graduate School faculty, as well as visiting lecturers who came to Nashville during the winter, also went to Blue Ridge in the summer. There they taught and lectured to P.W.G.'s and P.W.B.'s or to one of the many conferences.

Mrs. Weatherford ran their well-ordered home in Nashville and the pleasant summer cabin at Blue Ridge, sharing her husband's interest in the students. Whatever a student might need—funds, room, friendship—the Weatherfords stood ready to help provide it. One young man who was working his way through the Graduate School had gotten down to his last sixteen cents when Weatherford found him a job at the Wesley Hall cafeteria. Then Weatherford gave him work washing windows. The student was delighted that the soft coal smoke from Nashville furnaces kept the city dirty and the windows in need of frequent cleaning. When Weatherford also helped him secure the job of firing some of these furnaces, the boy was benefited both ways. To make sure that he could continue in school, the Weatherfords also invited him to live for a year in their home, which he did.

Their own son Willis was growing into a bright-eyed, gentle boy who went to Peabody Kindergarten and then to the Peabody Demonstration School. During the summers he was already beginning to undertake chores reminiscent of the strenuous outdoor life his father had known when he was growing up in Texas. Young Willis carried wood for use on chilly evenings in early and late summer, and when he grew a little older he learned to chop green logs and stack them in tall, neat ricks. Sometimes the wood supply seemed endless, but working with it was hardy discipline. It was also a healthy balance to the "book learning," as some of their mountain neighbors put it, which Willis had taken to so early and so easily.

One day in Nashville, Weatherford received a telephone call from a friend in New York. He described a Chinese student who was only newly arrived in this country but who was eager to have some American education. "What can you do for this man?" the friend asked.

"That's not the point," Weatherford answered. "What can he do for himself?" Then he invited his friend to send the Chinese student down.

So Li Tien Lee came to Nashville, and Weatherford soon realized that this was one of the brightest students he had ever had an opportunity to teach. Weatherford made certain during the next few years that Lee had a chance to complete his education in this country. After he had received his doctorate, Lee returned to China where he became head of the Young Men's Christian Association in that country. For many years he corresponded with Weatherford.

There were a few other foreign students at the Graduate School and a scattered representation from other regions of the United States, but the main body was made up of young Southerners who would, Weatherford hoped, work in the South.

"Dr. Weatherford's Graduate School was far ahead of its time," one of those students later recalled. "Its standards of high scholarship were especially in the vanguard. Dr. Weatherford was never associated with anything shoddy. He advocated skull-stretching work, both at the Graduate School and at Blue Ridge."

Skull-stretching work combined with heart-wrenching personal trouble early in this period. In the midst of participating in hikes and baking special pecan pie treats and arranging Sunday night suppers for and with the young ones at Nashville and Blue Ridge, Julia Weatherford fell ill. After numerous consultations and several uncertain diagnoses, doctors decided that her trouble was pleurisy. She was advised to go to Colorado.

The journey from Nashville to Colorado Springs was long and wearying. Weatherford found the recommended doctor and a semi-hospital situation where Mrs. Weatherford could receive treatment and rest for a few months. The months lengthened to a year, and one year stretched to three before she returned to her home, husband, and child.

During these years they went to her. Dr. Weatherford and Willis were in Colorado Springs for Christmases as well as those weeks between winter and summer terms and at the end of each summer school. During long walks they became familiar with the spectacular scenery of Colorado Springs and its vicinity. Yet the whole experience was a long, gruelling exercise in loneliness for these three people.

At home, Rosa Lea McKesson cared for the household needs of Willis and his father. A friend who went to have dinner with them in the midst of this troubled time did not know whether to stifle a smile or a sob when Willis —seven or eight years old—was asked to return thanks, sat very straight and began his blessing, "Lord, give us a man's work to do today."

But love, and necessity, brought them through the separation and illness. When Mrs. Weatherford returned home she seemed to be completely cured of her pleurisy condition. She resumed her personal participation in Blue Ridge summers and the high purposes of the Graduate School.

The Nashville Graduate School had come into being and continued to exist by the force of Weatherford's determination plus his energy in securing funds. Although he had been promised the assistance of those YMCA men who had urged him to accept this work, it was not long before Weatherford found that he was carrying almost the full load of financial responsibility. Rather than spend his time pleading for help, however, he found it easier, quicker, and more successful to spend time and energy going directly to the sources of funds.

Before long he had become a highly effective one-man team with almost a Midas touch for raising money for his school. His success brought with it major liabilities as well as gains, as later events would disclose. At the time, the chief negative result seemed to be an occasional antagonism on the part of others in the YMCA movement who felt that they were competing for some of that philanthropy and did not receive their share of donations.

One state secretary of the YMCA, for instance, had on his list of benefactors an iron works industrialist in his state who contributed an annual gift of fifty dollars to the Association. Weatherford went to see him and described the work of the Graduate School. His enthusiasm and personal commitment were contagious, and the industrialist gave him fifty thousand dollars for the college.

When the state secretary heard of this, he was not at all happy. He insisted that Weatherford should divide the gift with his state YMCA. Weatherford replied that he had no right to do this. His friend had made the donation specifically to the work of the Graduate School.

"Well, will you go with me to see him?" the disgruntled secretary demanded.

"Of course," Weatherford replied. They went to call on the philanthropist.

Weatherford's companion, however, was not equal to the moment. He hesitated, listed a few vague needs of his state YMCA and some even vaguer goals, and after a few minutes had completely lost this businessman's attention—and his donation.

Personal passion was the key to Weatherford's success, whether he was winning money or students. Commitment to Christianity by custom and tradition alone would always lead to an anemic, poverty-stricken religious life, he felt. Only personal passion could lift it—and the lives of those it affected—into a rare, rich plenty.

Such involvement, such lack of restraint in displaying deep emotion sometimes lifted Weatherford beyond more ordinary men and their efforts. In being set beyond them he became a target for their criticism as well as their approval, for misunderstanding as well as appreciation. There were those who thought his theology too liberal ("Why do religious leaders have to have all that education?"). Others found his racial ideas uncomfortable ("Our Negroes and white folks are getting along all right. Why doesn't he let things alone?"). Some scorned his insistence on scholarship; others damned with faint praise or hidden smirks his expenditures of physical and mental energy as he strove to make his prophecy of plenty come true. ("He couldn't realize some people are geared to a more moderate pace," one realist remarked.)

"He was a spellbinder," another of his students said,

"but he himself was spellbound, rapt, tireless, drawing superhuman strength from his spirituality."

There were those who called his determination doggedness and his enthusiasm impatience. But the majority opinion was later voiced by John R. Poteat, son of one of Weatherford's early Blue Ridge associates, when he said, "Dr. Weatherford combines the intelligence and integrity of the ivory tower with the efficiency of the man of action and the world of business."

Professors from Yale University's Divinity School came to the Nashville Graduate School and to Blue Ridge to participate in the program, and as they saw in action Weatherford's ideas for training religious leaders, they were impressed. Weatherford was invited to make a series of lectures at Yale. Following these lectures he was asked to join the Yale faculty as a full professor. He would teach courses in religious training.

Weatherford did not go to Yale. Through the years he would receive many attractive offers from other sections of the country. But somewhere in his youth he had become convinced of his mission in the South, and although work here might pay him less money or even less respect than he could have received elsewhere, he was determined to stay with his region. Not that his outlook was in any sense narrowly regional. On the contrary, it was broad enough to include the whole human race, and that was the outlook he wanted for his South, too.

Not long ago the president of an educational institution in California wrote Weatherford that many times as he wrestled with university administration he had recalled Weatherford's early work in building a faculty of broad religious influences, in advocating the necessity for higher caliber, well-trained men in the leadership of university programs. "On all these points and many others," he said, "you pioneered before the rest of us began thinking about them."

Weatherford's work at the Graduate School and in the many other undertakings owed its success perhaps most directly to his unembarrassed religious fervor combined with his practicality. This combination of qualities thrust him to the forefront in interracial and educational work in the South during the first half of the twentieth century. They are qualities he believes to be no less necessary in the latter half of this century. Confronted as we are with the possibility of massive death, the persistence of chronic poverty, tensions between new national independence and bonds of international interdependence, Weatherford asks how adjustments can be struck or solutions be found without commitment of morality as well as mechanics, without involvement of spirituality as well as sociology, without dedication of persons as well as pocketbooks.

Whatever task Weatherford entered upon, he brought it his total resources. Tasks accumulated faster than the years—and all of his resources were taxed, often, it seemed, to their limits.

14

Ability as an innovator sometimes overshadowed Weatherford's successes as a mediator. The patience he could exercise at a conference table, the courtesy and personal atmosphere of good will he brought to bear upon heated exchanges and delicate negotiations between opposite viewpoints were not as obvious as his more public characteristics. In church or interracial or educational fields where he labored, there was constant need for skillful and constructive mediation. Although Weatherford did not hesitate to bring down the meat cleaver if he found it the necessary weapon of change and justice, he did not fumble in wielding the scalpel if that seemed the appropriate instrument of progress with harmony.

One of his most influential contributions as a negotiator was made in 1923 to the YMCA. In an organization dedicated to leadership and at a convention attended only by the most select group of that leadership, Weatherford emerged on this occasion as one of the most respected and effective leaders of them all.

By 1923 the work of the YMCA had grown to such proportions that the state associations and the International Committee were in a crisis of conflict and confusion. "The basic question," historian Howard Hopkins has recorded, "was whether the two parallel organizations—state and International Committees—should continue to operate side by side or whether they ought to be joined either in one agency or with carefully delineated working relationships. Were state committees agents of the national Movement or independent entities?"

A Constitutional Convention was set for October, 1923, in Cleveland, Ohio, at which time it was hoped that an answer to this question might be determined and some order brought out of the existing chaos. When 1200 delegates finally assembled (one of the delegates was Franklin D. Roosevelt), a leading secretary and delegate described the situation at the Convention: "The extreme right apparently contended for absolute local and state autonomy with the national agency practically reduced to a few self-supporting Bureaus. The extreme left contended for a dominant, highly centralized leadership."

Between the "states' rights" group and the advocates of strong central control there seemed to be an unbridgeable gulf. If no definite action were taken, control would go by default to the separate state organizations. This, it seemed to Weatherford and a handful of other men present, would be an untenable situation. It would mean that forty-eight weak groups would be struggling along without any national unity. Efficient service to millions of young men and efficient use of millions of dollars were involved in this decision.

After the plan for local autonomy had been presented on the floor, behind-the-scenes work by Weatherford secured time and space on the agenda for presentation of a plan of integrated organization. This provided a choice to the delegates and gave rise to long and sometimes heated discussion on the floor.

In an effort to create the best organizational structure

possible and yet bring some measure of satisfaction to all conflicting viewpoints, Weatherford, W. W. Fry, and F. B. Shipp of Pittsburgh retired to a hotel suite and for three days and three nights worked at drafting such a plan.

When the three arbitrators came to the Convention hall and Weatherford mounted the platform to read the compromise proposals, the troubled audience was acutely attentive. As he finished reading the document they broke into applause—and then proceeded to question Weatherford and his committee for some three hours concerning details of this plan. Weatherford thought it was probably the most gruelling three hours of his life—but when the Convention voted its unanimous approval, the ordeal seemed worthwhile.

Weatherford described the compromise proposal that was adopted as "centralized organization with distributed responsibility." Both the International Committee and the state groups were satisfied that their work could go forward unhampered, yet oriented to the overall purposes. As one observer summed it up, "the organization now ceased being a crowd and became a unified Movement." One of the Association's publications said that the Movement had adopted "the form, furniture, and formulas of democracy." The plan worked out in Cleveland is essentially the structure—with modifications, of course—under which the YMCA functions today.

This Constitutional Convention at which Weatherford played such a crucial role was, in the opinion of many delegates, one of the greatest gatherings since the first meeting in 1854.

Less dramatic and decisive, of course, but even more important was Weatherford's continuing influence as interpreter between Negro and white Southerner. His efforts at mediation here could sometimes be brought to localized situations with clear-cut victories or defeats, but more often they were long-range and without a definite conclusion (unless a student's appreciative testimony could be weighed as one sort of conclusion: "You helped me become free of the terrible burden of prejudice and I shall be forever in your debt"). Such labors were slow and toilsome and drearily unpopular. Through the Commission on Interracial Cooperation he played a direct role in a few specific improvements and some large, more intangible gains. Through his books he sought to reach other people and hasten the slow educational process of understanding.

After his first two volumes on Negro life and Negro progress were published, several disturbing tracts began to circulate widely throughout the South. They were among the best known of an epidemic of such publications which came into being during the first part of the century. The first one Weatherford saw was entitled *The Passing of the Great Race* by Madison Grant. The second came a few years later: *The Rising Tide of Color Against White World-supremacy* by Theodore Lothrop Stoddard. Inflammatory and emotional, such books appealed to vague, half-buried fears. Salesmen peddled them from door to door in rural Southern counties and small towns where few book stores existed. Their message found its way into the thoughts and attitudes of people in many parts of the country. Weatherford had grown up in a farm community (where his mother had once bought a traveling salesman's book on the millennium), and he knew how influential such demagogic printed matter could be.

As an antidote to these wild publications, he wrote *The Negro from Africa to America*, which was published in 1924. In an introduction to this book, Dr. James Hardy Dillard declared that Weatherford had pioneered in showing white and Negro people how many vital interests were held in common. In this volume Weatherford examined some of the Negro's African background and discussed reasons for racial tensions in America. In 1965 Dr. George B. Tindall, in his essay for the collection entitled *Writing Southern History*, stated that *The Negro from Africa to America* "remains the best survey of Negro history by a white writer. The tone was that of history with a purpose."

Soon after *The Negro from Africa to America* was published, women's groups of the Methodist Church had selected sections of the book separately bound, and these were used as texts for home mission study classes.

A few years later the sociology department at Yale University asked Weatherford to choose a Negro co-author and write a college textbook on race relations. Weatherford asked Dr. Charles S. Johnson, head of the sociology department at Fisk University and later its president, to collaborate with him in producing such a volume.

When Johnson accepted, the two men met at Blue Ridge. There they worked out their chapter topics and selected the subjects each would cover. Johnson took fifteen chapters to write, and Weatherford took fourteen plus the bibliography, index, and list of topics for special study.

Before work began, however, Weatherford said to his associate, "We are not interested in a book that is the least common denominator of two minds." Johnson agreed wholeheartedly as he did to Weatherford's subsequent proposal that they exchange manuscripts, when each was ready, and make any criticisms that seemed justified.

In the course of writing this text the two authors had some frank and sharp exchanges, but each respected the other's reputation for scholarship and just appraisal. When each of them finally read the manuscript in full, Weatherford voiced his approval of Johnson's chapters, and Johnson said to Weatherford in true professorial vernacular, "I want to give you three A's: one for research, one for clear writing and the other one for fair-mindedness." Weatherford was as pleased as he had once been when he received a high grade at Weatherford College or Vanderbilt.

In 1934 *Race Relations* by Weatherford and Johnson was published. It was adopted as a text by more than sixty colleges and almost as many graduate schools. Some of these were in the South, a fact which especially pleased the authors.

In his introduction to the book, Jerome Davis of Yale said: "The authors of this book are leaders in the attempt to work out a basis for intelligent and mutually tolerant relations between the two races . . . . Proceeding on the theory that knowledge begets sympathy, they analyze and discuss factually and candidly various aspects of the problem of race relations between whites and Negroes in the United States, relying on the historical, sociological, and statistical data which they adduce, to prove their contention that 'sweeping generalizations about either race are apt to be largely false.' They do not minimize the difficulties confronting both the whites and Negroes in their relationships and they propose no easy solutions; they do, however, explode many popular fallacies, and it is safe to say that if every community could approach the problem in the spirit of the authors of this volume, much of the problem itself would be well on the way to adjustment."

For their part, Weatherford and Johnson concluded that "So far as the writers know, no textbook in sociology has heretofore been undertaken by a white man and a Negro as joint authors. It is their hope that others may try a similar task. What we need at present is more opportunities for white and colored to undertake common tasks, for the final desideration of understanding is cooperation. They therefore send this book out as a concrete expression of racial cooperation and, they believe, of racial good will and understanding."

In the years between publication of these two books Weatherford took another step to further his concrete influence on Southern racial progress. He became a member of the Board of Directors of American Cast Iron Pipe Company in Birmingham, Alabama, in 1927.

As noted previously, this company was unique in its aims and in its organization, and both its uniqueness and its success were due to the vision of its founder, John J. Eagan of Atlanta.

Eagan was five years older than Weatherford, having been born in Griffin, Georgia, in 1870. While he was an infant his father died and left him and his twenty-five-year-old mother in moderate circumstances. At an early age he went to work for his uncle, William A. Russell, and upon the death of Mr. Russell, twenty-nine-year-old John J. Eagan found himself in possession of a considerable fortune. With this money he helped organize the American Cast Iron Pipe Company, called ACIPCO, in October, 1905. Until his death in 1924 he remained in charge of the company, either as president or as chairman of the Board of Directors. His interests were humanitarian as well as financial, and he took active leadership in the Presbyterian Church, in the YMCA, in education (he was on the Board of Trustees of the Martha Berry Schools of Georgia for many years and through this service made a contribution to education of mountain youth), and in race relations. It was inevitable that Eagan and Weatherford should cross paths.

The two men first met when Weatherford called upon Eagan in his office in Atlanta in 1919. Eagan told his visitor that he had just hired a man to be in charge of social work for the ACIPCO plant, and the first question he had asked this new employee was whether he had read W. D. Weatherford's *Negro Life in the South.*

Weatherford's writings influenced the industrialist and was a factor in Eagan's decision to join the Commission on Interracial Cooperation, which was founded later that year. Eagan had long sustained a concern for all of the people working in his plant, however, and because a large percentage of his employees were Negroes he had become involved in racial problems.

One freedom enjoyed by ACIPCO that was not available to many similar industries of the period was freedom from the handicap of absentee ownership. A unique feature of ACIPCO's history was that it was financed totally by Southern capital. This fact was most important in allowing Eagan to develop his famous Eagan Plan.

The first step toward this plan came with Mr. Eagan's offer, early in the history of the plant, to give employees an interest in company gains by awarding ten shares of stock in the company to any employee who remained with ACIPCO for five consecutive years. This was followed by housing, recreational, and educational innovations for employees, all far ahead of their time in industrial Birmingham. Then in July, 1922, Eagan announced that company profits would be shared with all employees on a cash basis. This early profit sharing and equally progressive procedures of employee representation put Eagan and ACIPCO in the vanguard of enlightened industrial relations. He took his message of Christian principles applied in the modern business world to the Industrial Relations Conferences at Blue Ridge.

When he died in March, 1924, it was discovered that he had placed all of the common stock of ACIPCO in trust, and the profits from this trust were to be used for the benefit of all the company's employees. "By this codicil to my will and testament," he wrote, "it is my purpose, will and desire to create a trust estate both for the benefit of the persons actually in the employ of said American Cast Iron Pipe Company, and for such persons as may require the products of said Company."

The policies and conduct of business of ACIPCO from that day forward have been regulated by a Board of Directors composed of representatives of the public, employees, managers, and owners. The first person from outside who was elected to this Board following John Eagan's death was his widow. The second person elected was Weatherford. From 1927 to the present he has represented the employees of ACIPCO. Of some 162 Board meetings during those years he has attended 158. Almost without exception he has opened the meeting with a prayer, and on each occasion he has repeated this supplication: "Remind us afresh that our purpose is people first and pipe second."

Successful manufacture of pipe has been the means by which ACIPCO could help people, however, and Weatherford has been as mindful of this fact as any other member of the company. Today ACIPCO is the largest individual cast-iron pressure-pipe manufacturing plant in the world. Of its 2100 employees approximately one-fifth have been with the company a quarter of a century or longer. With some 45 per cent of its work force Negro, this company has one of the lowest rates of worker turnover in the industry, for its Eagan Plan and its policies have not only brought prosperity; they have also brought a sense of worker-participation which is one aspect of a plant's prosperity. During a period of financial depression when the company was struggling for survival, one of its men wrote, "Economy is a thing of the spirit. Sometimes a workman, because he believes his company rich, wastes time and materials. He thinks it comes out of the other man's pocket. Here that spirit injures him as much as anyone else."

On the ACIPCO Board, Weatherford's combination of idealism and practicality has again been in evidence. One of the first occasions on which he spoke up at a directors' meeting involved a decision on the pipe-making process. What did this educator, minister, scholar know about pipe? Weatherford had made some study of the subject. If he were going to be responsible in any measure for the success of this industry, he would not allow ignorance of its product to blight his effectiveness. He had gone into the plant; he had asked questions and talked with the laborers and the foremen and the management. He knew what this vote on ACIPCO's developing its own centrifugal pipe-making process involved: familiar methods, security, and the status quo versus risk and progress. He made a motion for ACIPCO to develop the new process.

In dealing with fellow members of the Board he could provide outspoken leadership. At one point in the company's development when the president had adopted dictatorial methods in an effort to impose one-man rule on an industry whose whole philosophy was one of carefully conceived and constructed cooperation, it was Weatherford who gave voice to the general discontent. His courage was inspired by the good of the company as a whole. Year after year that company became a more and more personal entity to him, a growing list of names and faces and families whose work was familiar—in the Board room, at the furnaces, in the machine shop. After Weatherford had spoken, others followed; this particular official was asked to resign from ACIPCO.

As a member of the wages committee, Weatherford had particular need of his common sense. In addition to the profits which were divided among employees, bonuses also began to accrue. During the past twenty-one years some fifteen million dollars in bonus wages has been paid to ACIPCO employees. When these payments first began, however, they were made annually, in one lump sum. Then it was discovered that this led many of the employees to unwise purchasing practices. Down payments were often made on expensive luxury items which then kept the family budget drained by monthly payments. As a result, bonuses are now paid quarterly.

When Kenneth Daniel, current president of ACIPCO, was five years old, he met Dr. Weatherford. Daniel came to Blue Ridge during many summers, climbed its mountains, played in its gym, and went swimming in its pool in "the coldest water in the world." Today their relationship is a fine combination of warm friendliness and cool business.

"If we don't make profits, we don't realize our ideals," Daniel says, "and Dr. Weatherford is a constant source of sound advice and wise criticism. If you think he sits quietly by when he sees something wrong, you don't know Dr. Weatherford.

"We have 350 acres in our plant and when he comes to a Board meeting he can walk over most of it and still make you trot to keep up with him. He can talk with men along the way and sense their mood immediately. It means a great deal to the president of a company to sit down four times a year and talk with a man like this. Many things can be substituted, but not ninety years of living!"

One of Weatherford's biggest satisfactions at ACIPCO has been its practical contribution to race relations. The situation is not ideal and no realistic person would contend that a Negro's chances for promotion are equal to a white workman's chances even today, but opportunities approach the ideal more closely than in most other similar corporations. Good pay and distribution of profits and bonuses and a voice in the company's operation all contributed to the fact that when the big migrations

North began to drain away some of the South's Negro labor, ACIPCO's Negro work force remained relatively steady.

A lawyer who is a fellow member of the ACIPCO Board has remarked of Weatherford: "I won't say he's the greatest Christian I've ever known, but I will say he works harder at applying Christianity in daily life than any man I've ever known."

It is easy to write and speak about lofty ethical and religious principles. It is less easy to apply those principles in the hurly-burly of professional or business careers. It is perhaps most difficult of all to embrace those principles so completely that they become part of private life, too, infusing even intimate family relationships with something approaching grandeur. It has been observed that no man is a hero to his valet (or to his wife or secretary?). This presupposes that heroism is a momentary flash of splendor, a pinnacle experience that cannot be sustained over the long weary haul of time and daily distractions. Weatherford was not one to urge spiritual riches on others and then through either conscious or unconscious hypocrisy leave his own and his family's spirit poverty stricken. And in 1933 they had need of all the spiritual strength their frail humanity could muster.

Julia Weatherford was under a doctor's care again, but after a long period of many hours of rest each day she became well enough to spend most of her time downstairs with her family, and she could even participate in some outside activities. While she was recovering, Weatherford underwent an operation for hernia. One day after he had returned from the hospital a neighbor called to complain about their son Willis' dog, which had caused some slight disturbance in the neighborhood. When the dog, a big friendly shepherd, was located, he seemed to be acting strangely and he was put under observation. When Dr. Weatherford told his surgeon of the incident, the doctor said that all those who had had contact with the dog should take anti-rabies shots. Mrs. Weatherford protested that she had not been bitten or even scratched; she did not want to take the treatment. But following her husband's and doctor's counsel, she drove the neighbor and her daughter, and Willis and herself, to the doctor to begin the long series of twenty-one shots.

After the thirteenth shot, Mrs. Weatherford became desperately ill. She lost consciousness and was rushed to the hospital where for weeks she hovered between life and death. Hallucinations filled her days and nights. Old-timers would have called it brain fever.

At last, however she regained consciousness. Thin and pale almost beyond recognition, she at first seemed too weak to move. Then, the fact of her paralysis became apparent to herself and to those around her.

From that day forward Julia Weatherford had no use of her body from the waist down. Gradually she regained some use of her arms and hands and control of her head and face, but after a period of progress and determined optimism these muscles began to slip once more from her control. For twenty-four years this woman who had been so fastidious about her home and her family's welfare, who had enjoyed her flowers and pretty clothes and hikes in the woods and athletics with young people, would have to endure separation from that world. Her effort to make the separation appear unimportant was valiant. But the suffering was there, behind the mask.

There, too, and even more terrible in its own way, was the anguish of the one whose solicitude had brought on this disaster. The daily sight of his "dear girl's" helplessness was a wound that refused to heal, but Weatherford accepted it and then sought a palliative through complete dedication to her smallest comfort and delight. He anticipated her needs, found various ways to demonstrate his affection, and provided a quiet strength on which she could lean. During those twenty-four years he pushed on in contributing a man's portion to the work of the world, but he did not neglect the most trivial detail of his wife's schedule or her desires.

At first, Julia Weatherford found it difficult to reconcile herself to a life which would always be at the mercy (and pity) of others. She was a proud woman and a participator in life—although she had always had that indefinable air of reserve which is frequently the characteristic of queens—and she could not endure the thought of being a burden to those she loved for the rest of her life. She experienced a time of bitterness. She touched bottom. Then gradually she began to swim up through the deeps toward light again. And the main source of that light was her family, husband and son.

She looked at her son, now a tall, slim student at Vanderbilt achieving an outstanding record. In many ways his looks and his character were hers. She saw that she had much to be proud of, and her despair was lessened.

She looked at her husband. He was engaged in a multitude of activities. His ideas did not cease coming, his energy did not flag, his vision of plenty could not be diminished. But he, too, had need of her love—and of her faith which would reveal her own reconciliation to the tragedy.

15

Blows did not fall singly or lightly in Weatherford's life. His Julia had been stricken in 1933, and during the years immediately afterward they spent time and money and immense resources of hope in visits to various doctors. In 1936 Weatherford took his wife to a neurosurgeon in New York. While they remained there for several months, Weatherford put on his last tremendous push to raise funds for his Graduate School in Nashville.

One of the great commitments of Weatherford's life, the college, which had been in existence for seventeen years, was in its last days. This time he had little success in his search for money—too few people were giving too little money to anyone in 1936. Apparently unsuccessful in finding a cure for his wife's paralysis or his school's economic crisis, Weatherford returned to Nashville. Later that year, Southern YMCA Graduate School was closed.

The Graduate School's success in raising standards of scholarship in religious leaders for the South was attested to by students and outside observers alike. "It opened our eyes to the relevance of religion in the world today," a graduate would testify years later.

The knowledgeable executive director of the Rosenwald Fund in Chicago, Edwin Embree, who kept in close touch with educational and racial progress in the South, had said that the only two institutions he knew that were doing really effective work on the race question were the Vanderbilt Medical School and the YMCA Graduate School. (The Graduate School was the first in the United States to require a course on race relations.)

The testimony of one student was echoed by many others when he said, "Science is wonderful in its teaching and development of ways to measure material things. I wish there was some kind of measuring stick that would accurately record the influence Weatherford had on my life and the lives of others who have come in contact with him."

A few years after the Graduate School closed, 80 per cent of all the student YMCA secretaries in Southern colleges and universities were found to be its graduates. One official from the New York office would report, after a trip through the South, that wherever anything significant was happening a man from the Graduate School was in charge.

Why then had this school, successful in many ways, been forced to close? What had brought about this keenest disappointment of Weatherford's professional career? The reason was three-fold.

First, although the school was possessed of a half-million dollar plant, the problem of obtaining the hundred thousand dollars necessary for each year's budget grew increasingly difficult. The great depression had tightened its grip on the economic life of America, and because the South was the poorest region in the country, it was also the most cruelly hurt by financial panic. The income and activities of the Southern YMCA's that were supposed to support the college had dwindled, and by 1936 their contributions amounted to only one-sixteenth of the annual budget for the school. Only Weatherford's persistent efforts had kept the college alive this long. But as a second wave of recession began to stir across the country, even these efforts were not sufficient. The Graduate School became one of the victims of the depression.

Second, the Graduate School had not enjoyed the support that might have been expected from lay leadership and state secretaries of the YMCA across the South. Their attitude was summed up in the reaction of one state secretary who said, when Weatherford warned that he could not carry the whole financial burden of the Graduate School any longer: "Well, maybe it's just as well to close it down. I don't know that we need all that education."

Such attitudes and Weatherford's thoughts were a million light years apart. And perhaps Weatherford had done too little to span that gulf over the years. As long as his dedication and verve had carried others along with him, he had had neither the time nor the inclination to cultivate their approval. When the showdown came and that approval was desirable, and their support indispensable, it did not come through. Perhaps this was one time when Weatherford's advanced leadership had put him so far ahead of his associates that they lost sight of him.

Third, Vanderbilt University, under the leadership of its devoted Chancellor James H. Kirkland, showed surprisingly little generosity of spirit (and considerable shrewdness of mind) in its swift foreclosure on the Graduate School. Vanderbilt held a mortgage in the amount of $155,000 upon the half-million dollar facilities of the Graduate School. The Chancellor did not delay unduly in his foreclosure but obeyed the law to its last letter. His former student and later colleague, W. D. Weatherford, made no reproaches about this procedure, then or ever after, but there were loyal friends of both Kirkland's and Weatherford's who felt that upon this occasion the old Chancellor had revealed some qualities that made Weatherford's usual forcefulness and even abruptness seem dawdling playfulness by comparison.

Nearly two decades of effort at the Graduate School were finished. But as Weatherford's close associates knew and one said, "He could always close the door on anything that was past. When he lost the Graduate School it must have been a cruel blow, but I never heard him remark on it. He was already facing up to the next thing."

"The next thing" in this case was Fisk University in Nashville. When the Graduate School became part of Vanderbilt University in 1936, Dr. Thomas Elsa Jones, Northern-born, white, Quaker president of Fisk University, asked Weatherford to join his faculty.

The opportunity to work with Negro students, to learn their problems at first-hand, and to make such contribution as he could to the enrichment of their lives was irresistible. There was also the challenge of refuting many white myths and prejudices. Although the South had never disavowed its responsibility to include Negroes in the public school system, much of the attitude toward higher education would have agreed with the opinion often voiced that "an educated Negro is a good plowhand spoiled."

One of the department heads at Vanderbilt asked Weatherford why he was going to Fisk to teach. "Because I've been interested in the race question for a long time and this is a chance to see what I can do about it," Weatherford replied.

"Queer," his friend said as he turned away, "the choices some people make."

The university Weatherford had chosen to work in was one of the many Southern Negro colleges born between 1865 and 1870 of the marriage of Northern religion-philanthropy and the U. S. Freedmen's Bureau.

178

Weatherford himself later recorded, in his book *American Churches and the Negro,* one little episode in Fisk's beginnings as reported in an 1866 Cincinnati *Gazette.* The scene was the famous Belle Meade estate of General Harding. "Yesterday General Fisk went out to General Harding's to talk to him and the colored people about a school. When the matter was first broached Mr. Harding expressed himself in strong terms against it. . . . However, a meeting was called and General Harding introduced General Fisk, told who he was, what his business was, and sat down. . . . After hearing the General and beholding the enthusiasm of the blacks, Mr. Harding gracefully surrendered."

Fisk enjoyed a high academic reputation from the start. In 1869, only three years after it was established, the general agent of the Peabody Fund reported that he found it the best normal school he had seen in the South. From the standpoint of Weatherford's subsequent association with both schools, it is interesting to note that this agent also went on to recommend that an appropriation be given Fisk in preference to Berea College, which at that time enrolled both Negro and white students.

The university had come into national and international prominence early in the 1870's when a group called the "Fisk Jubilee Singers" was organized. Although one newspaper reporter called them "General Fisk's Nigger Minstrels," crowned heads of Europe and leaders in all parts of America were captivated by this band of ex-slaves who sang their own spirituals and work-songs and other music with such feeling and talent. When Mark Twain had heard them sing in Switzerland, he declared that the loveliest memory of his European travels was hearing these old plantation melodies. Jubilee Hall, the central building on the Fisk campus, had been built with the money earned by these singers.

In the continuing debate over whether education for

Negroes should be "classical" or "industrial," Fisk—as opposed to schools such as Tuskegee Institute with its outstanding vocational program—had maintained its position as a liberal arts school. (Helen Clarissa Morgan, one of the first teachers at Fisk, had come from Oberlin to discover that her first Latin classes would meet in a dirt-floored barracks abandoned by the Army.) The point of view which advocated broad liberal education for Negroes had been stated by the brilliant and embittered W. E. B. DuBois, a Fisk graduate who took his doctorate at Harvard in 1895: "The Negro race is going to be saved by its exceptional men . . . if we make money the object of man-training, we shall make money-makers but not necessarily men; if we make technical skill the object of education, we may possess artisans but not, in nature, men."

Weatherford knew both DuBois and Booker T. Washington, who, with his vocational success at Tuskegee, stood at the opposite pole of this educational controversy. Weatherford and Washington were friends, but friendship with DuBois was difficult. Weatherford tried to understand DuBois' mordant mind, however, when he heard of the incident at the funeral for DuBois' child. A white passer-by had said, in the father's hearing, as the small casket was carried down the street, "It's only a nigger baby."

Weatherford went to Fisk as head of the Department of Religion and Philosophy. There was one professor in the department. Many of the teachers in the university seemed to him to have a somewhat casual attitude toward grading and toward the general achievement level of their students. Many of the students appeared to need understanding at a cultural as well as an academic level. As a small but meaningful illustration, Weatherford soon discovered that some of his students chewed gum. At the end of the first week he made the remark in class one day that no cultured lady or gentleman ever chewed gum in public. This reminder worked so well that Weatherford used it for several seasons as the best way to handle this particular little problem.

Larger problems—and satisfactions—came with his work on changing the curriculum. The president and certain members of the faculty asked him to prepare an introductory course in the humanities. This was the first such course offered at Fisk or any other Negro college. Within a short while it became a required subject for all sophomores, approximately one hundred and fifty a year. Weatherford was given a student reader-assistant for each of the three classes of this course, and through these choice students he became yet better acquainted with Fisk.

One such reader was the daughter of his old friend, Dr. Charles S. Johnson, head of the Department of Sociology. Patricia Johnson was a bright, beautiful girl whose previous education had been in private Catholic schools, the best her parents found available to her. She first encountered Dr. Weatherford in his humanities course. Because she was quick and intelligent, she thought it would be easy to slide by in such a subject, and she did not bother to get a copy of the text Weatherford recommended, James Henry Breasted's *Ancient Times*. She listened attentively to his classroom lectures —rich in content and delivered in a clear crisp style— but she did not feel it necessary to undertake much outside reading. When her first grades began to register failure, however, she was shocked. After an interview with Dr. Weatherford, she began to find time to read both in the assigned text and in other books, and she discovered that the subject was fascinating. She discovered, too, that the tests were not fiendish riddles at all but clear and meaningful questions. At the end of that term she made an *A* and was asked to serve as a student assistant.

Patricia Johnson later explained that this initial encounter with Dr. Weatherford taught her the value of that asset he had imparted to many other Southern students: academic discipline. Her subsequent work with him brought her religious and philosophic insight. She did not find him an easy person to know, but she drew upon qualities she felt were more important—his kindness, sympathy, and understanding. Perhaps it was that rare combination of academic discipline *and* warm personal understanding that made Weatherford's work with college students both unique and effective.

During his first months at Fisk there were those Negroes in the university community who felt that his attitude was somewhat paternalistic. They resented this. Gradually, however, most of them came to realize that this attitude had nothing to do with race. Weatherford was paternalistic, on occasion, to anyone or everyone who came under his stern, loving, all-giving, all-demanding care.

As he stood before his classes day after day and worked with his colleagues term after term—almost invariably wearing a dark well-pressed suit and white shirt, his white hair meticulously parted—the influence of his character as revealed in that appearance began to have effect. His courses in religion and humanities began to be almost as popular as the outstanding sociology studies which had made Dr. Johnson the most popular professor at Fisk. Weatherford was asked by the Chaplain to speak three or four times a year at the Sunday morning services, more than any other member of the faculty or even the president of the university.

The meaning—perhaps the necessity—of his presence

here was made clear to Weatherford one day by an exchange he had with one of the students. He had become aware of a sort of caste system that seemed to operate among some of the girls on campus, a caste determined by the lightness or darkness of skin. Few very black boys or girls seemed to be elected to class offices. The most bitter, however, because of their ambivalent social position, were often the fair-complexioned ones. One such girl was from Boston. As Weatherford spoke to one of his classes on the development of religious thought, he stated that no person could harbor hatred of other people and be a true follower of Jesus and his teachings.

When the class was over, Weatherford found the girl from Boston waiting for him as he left the classroom. She repeated his statement and asked if that was what he had said. Weatherford told her it was.

"Then I can't be a Christian," she blurted out, "because I hate people. I hate all white people!"

Weatherford tried to show no shock at this assault. "No," he said, "no you don't."

She looked at him defiantly.

"I'm white—but I don't believe you hate me."

"Oh no. I know you!"

Each year Fisk sponsored a Fine Arts Festival, and the year that Weatherford was asked to serve as chairman of the committee arranging this festival he determined to feature once more the indigenous music that had been somewhat shunted aside through the years. He made a trip to Washington where he found Alan Lomax (son of Weatherford's former professor, John A. Lomax), curator of folk music and materials at the Library of Congress. Weatherford told Lomax his plan and the latter sent much interesting source material from which the program was built. A gifted member of the music department composed a cantata for the occasion. That part of the Festival brought an overflow crowd to the auditorium and was one of the most memorable evenings Weatherford experienced while he was at Fisk.

One of the needs Weatherford had found throughout his life was that for a better educated ministry, and once again he turned his attention to this field. He wanted his teaching to have an impact beyond the formal classroom and the boundaries of the college; he wanted it to reach out and touch the broader community. So he and Dr. Faulkner of the religion department organized a three-hour weekly class for Negro ministers who occupied pulpits in or near Nashville. Some fifty-eight of these men came each week to study philosophy of religion under Weatherford, church organization under Faulkner, and introduction to philosophy under a man who had recently come from Yale. A few of these ministers drove from rural areas as far as forty miles each way. Frequently they asked Weatherford to come and preach at their churches, and through these experiences Weatherford broadened his understanding of Negro talents and needs.

While he was teaching at Fisk in the winter, Weatherford was also running Blue Ridge during the summer. At the same time he was participating to the limit of his abilities in the other institutions and organizations he had joined or helped found (the Interracial Commission, ACIPCO, Berea College). His wife's illness was the focal point of his personal life, of course. Her condition demanded patience, and Weatherford had to cultivate that virtue even as he learned to restrain his hope of finding a cure for her paralysis. His schedule of work with others and care for Julia stretched endurance thin.

In 1943 a committee representing the YMCA's of the South approached Weatherford with a proposal that the Blue Ridge property be turned over to the Southern Associations. Weatherford welcomed the suggestion. Some of his closest friends and associates were on the committee, and he felt this was an appropriate time to transfer responsibility to others. Again, as at the Graduate School, he had been carrying a disproportionate amount of the fund-raising duties for Blue Ridge. World War II had brought further difficulties for all conference centers, too. With two stipulations which were readily accepted—that the YMCA's would secure money to retire a $74,000 indebtedness and make needed improvements, and that they would continue to use Blue Ridge as a religious training center for the people of the South—Weatherford turned Blue Ridge over to the new committee representing the Associations. Blue Ridge—with its long tree-lined drive of pine sentinels, its white-columned Lee Hall and spacious verandas, its wild acres of unspoiled mountain woods and streams—was perhaps of all his many undertakings closest to Weatherford's heart. But he was not abandoning it now, only allowing it to be adopted by others, and in 1944 he severed official ties with Blue Ridge.

Two years later he resigned from the faculty of Fisk University. He was approaching his seventy-first birthday. The administration of the university offered to waive the usual retirement requirements if he would stay on the faculty. This did not seem wise to Weatherford, however, and he foresaw the possibility of dissatisfaction on the part of other teachers if he accepted this special dispensation.

He had been at Fisk ten years. There were now five professors in his Department of Religion and Philosophy. He had performed the wedding ceremony for Dr. Faulkner's daughter when she was married shortly before his resignation. The rural ministers with whom he had worked in the special evening class presented him with a Bible and a eulogy that "scraped the stars." And several hundred students had learned the drudgery and joy, the slavery and mastery that were part of academic discipline—and this was one aspect of self-discipline.

As he prepared to leave Fisk, Berea College offered Weatherford a new opportunity, a new call to be a prophet of plenty among those mountain people he had respected and loved for so long.

16

In 1946 Weatherford, who had refused a call to become president of Berea in an earlier year, joined the staff of the college in a rather special capacity. He was seventy-one years old, ready to move his total professional commitment as well as his personal life into the heart of Southern Appalachia, with all of its breathtaking beauty and its heartbreaking problems.

His responsibility to his wife prompted efforts that approached the heroic. "She needs all I can provide for her," he sometimes explained to friends who exclaimed at his whirlwind pace, and he did not refer only to material comforts but also to the minutest daily attentiveness he could bestow. His responsibility to the mountain people also seemed clear to him and demanded his best efforts. Colleagues at Berea have remarked on his acceptance of each of these responsibilities, not as back-breaking burdens to be borne but as joyous opportunities to be fulfilled. Maintenance of this attitude was perhaps one of Weatherford's finest achievements.

In 1940, six years before his decision to work for Berea, he and Mrs. Weatherford (she a partial invalid then for seven years but still ready to contribute her tasteful guidance to all the exterior plans and interior appointments) had finished building a home on Overlook, a steep ridge behind the Blue Ridge Assembly. There, 3200 feet in the sky, with a panorama of plunging valleys and soaring pinnacles—twenty peaks over 5000 feet tall—stretched before them, they had built the quintessence of a mountain home and named it, in an inspired moment, Far Horizons.

They used native materials from their own 185 acres: river-worn stone and poplar logs for the walls, white oak with maple pegs for the floors, black walnut for interior panelling of halls, living room, and library, mountain stone for a big fireplace. They employed neighbor artisans in the construction and achieved a spacious, unpretentious, unique home. Building in such an unusual location posed problems, of course. When the local electric and telephone companies almost flatly refused to attempt to scale the mountainside, they reckoned without Weatherford's persistence. Again and again he returned to their offices, reminding them of past agreements made when he was director of Blue Ridge, pointing out routes which the lines might conveniently follow. Power and phone came up the mountain. Water came down from a private reservoir filled by cold springs.

Far Horizons became their permanent residence, and Weatherford divided his time between North Carolina, Berea, and any other place—from New York to Sandy Mush Creek, from Chicago to Shut-In—where he could do something constructive for mountain education.

Their son was embarked on his own life. Academic studies brought him, in addition to his B.A. degree from Vanderbilt, a Bachelor of Divinity from Yale and an M.A. and Ph.D. in economics from Harvard. Work for the American Friends Service Committee and the United States government took him to Egypt, Western Europe, Malaya, and India for periods ranging from one to two years.

With Willis gone and her husband frequently away from Far Horizons as he pursued his work, Julia Weatherford had to rely heavily on the hired couples who came to live in the lower story of their two-level house and to care for her and the home. A procession of such couples over the years provided her with drama, friendship, conflict, humor, and irritation. In one experience the husband proved to be a drug addict. At another time a wife fifteen years older than her husband proved to be so totally incapable that the whole experience bordered on the hilarious. Occasionally a pair could be found who would bring both order and an atmosphere of serenity, and then the arrangement might settle down for a comparatively long period. Such human relations problems might seem trivial to an outsider, but they revealed the daily and total dependence of Julia Weatherford. They called for all the patience and laughter and generosity of spirit she could muster, but she was possessed of these qualities in abundance. And although she could no longer be physical manager of her home, she could remain its spiritual mistress, making sure that it was an oasis of gracious manners (linen tablecloths and dinner napkins at every meal), light and comfort (no detail of fresh flowers, embroidered towels, a current book placed at a convenient spot too small to receive her attention)—an oasis for her son, her husband, and a constant flow of friends.

The road to Far Horizons was well graded, but it was steep and narrow. It might frighten visitors sometimes, but it seldom seemed to deter them. Someone who had been impressed by the number of people who came to Far Horizons each week asked Weatherford: "If this many people come to see you on this mountain top, how many more do you suppose you'd have had if you had built in an accessible spot?"

"No more," Weatherford replied. "Probably no one

would have come to see us then. It's the climb and the view that challenges them."

Despite his constant concern with his wife's welfare at home, the daily letter or telephone call when he was absent, Weatherford took up his new work for Berea with the methodical zeal and sense of mission he had brought to previous undertakings. His task was two-fold. First, he would recruit money for the college's sustenance and enlargement, and this would take him, for the most part, out of the mountains. Second, he would recruit worthy students for Berea, and this would take him deep into the most remote counties in the mountains. The latter work was his favorite, a culmination for which all his other efforts were mere groundwork.

Francis Hutchins, son of former president William J. Hutchins, was now president of Berea. Weatherford and William J. had become close friends as well as educational allies during the years after Weatherford had joined the Berea Board. Many times they had spent a whole day away from the interruptions and pressures of office, riding horseback through the woods and hills beyond the college. As they rode they shared problems, hopes, plans for a common goal: a richer life (and that meant better education) for the mountain people. This former close association made the later relationship between Weatherford and the younger Hutchins both easier and more difficult. It bred mutual respect and devotion—and also an occasional paternalistic approach on the part of Weatherford that might have irritated a man of less gentleness and insight than Hutchins. He and Weatherford understood that they were bound together by a great common goal.

When Weatherford published, in 1955, a book called *Educational Opportunities in the Appalachian Mountains*, Hutchins wrote a statement for Berea College in which he set forth a program and purpose that coincided remarkably with Weatherford's own personal aims and convictions. He also pointed out facts which would direct the course of Weatherford's next monumental project.

"Berea believes itself to be unique in at least three respects," Hutchins wrote. "First, it is dedicated to the education of the youth of two hundred and thirty southern Appalachian counties. These people are of prevailing Scotch-English blood, and ninety-nine and one-tenth per cent of them go back seven and eight generations on American soil. . . . Ninety per cent of Berea's students are chosen from these two hundred and thirty mountain counties. The forebears of these people had been hidden away in these mountains for nearly three hundred years, and few people in America know anything about their sterling worth.

"The second characteristic of Berea which we believe makes it unique is that Berea charges no tuition and never has in its hundred years of existence. The reason for this is that there are thousands of boys and girls in the mountains who have good brains and fine character, but little or no money. . . .

"The U.S. Government had a survey made of these mountain counties some years ago and reported that the average total income of a rural Appalachian family was $764. You just cannot send children to college on that amount of income. When Berea charges no tuition it virtually gives every boy and girl who matriculates a scholarship of $503 each year, for that is the educational cost to Berea for libraries, laboratories, teachers, etc. We do not knowingly take any student who is able to go to a college where he pays tuition. Neither do we take students with less than a B grade record.

"The third thing which makes Berea unique is that we have a labor program designed to give educational values in all work done. Our theory of labor is not that labor is a means of making money to get an education, but it is educational in itself if properly undertaken and properly supervised. Thus, we have fifteen hand industries on the campus where sophomores, juniors, and seniors may work and learn while they earn. We believe if we can teach boys and girls promptness, accuracy, speed, creative imagination, a sense of responsibility to their job, and thorough dependability on the job, that these qualities will be as valuable in after years as anything they learn in the library, laboratory, or the classroom. . . .

"Finally, it should be said that Berea's concern is not alone for its fifteen hundred students. We consider it our opportunity and our obligation to help transform the life of the whole mountain area."

Weatherford became intimately acquainted with the wide reach of Berea's work, from its woodworking shop to its language classes, from its weaving rooms to its musical concerts. He appreciated the old designs and patterns that were preserved and perpetuated in the coverlets, cloths, materials that poured from the busy looms, and the native woods—black walnut, richly grained cherry—that went into the furniture and smaller carvings from the carpentry shop. Knowing the variety of Berea's contribution to the total life of the mountains, he could better persuade outsiders to make a financial contribution to Berea. It was his first-hand knowledge of the need that made his approach to fundraising effective.

Weatherford felt that most of those with whom he talked in New York and other cities were somewhat like Berea's librarian, Dr. Elisabeth Peck, when she first came to Berea. She had arrived in September, 1912, and after a little while in the Kentucky hills had decided she didn't like the place very well. Her hard-earned Ph.D. degree was brand new and she was extremely proud of it, but Berea wasn't in an area where such an academic trophy garnered much respect. At last she went to Dr. Frost, then president of the college, and told him she wanted to be released from her two-year contract and given an honorable discharge. President Frost said he would give her back her contract and write a favorable recommendation. There was one condition, however. Before she left she would have to go back into the mountains for two months and become acquainted with mountain people.

Dr. Peck had no choice. So she went into the Kentucky hills and stayed at different homes, sometimes with the families of Berea students, sometimes with strangers. One family especially impressed her. They lived near Harlan, deep in the coal-mining, feuding back-country, and Dr. Peck entered into the family's activities. She helped peddle vegetables, taught Sunday School, and preached on one or two occasions when the minister didn't appear for services.

After two months she returned to Berea and went to Dr. Frost's office. "I'm here to stay," she announced. "You can't run me off!"

Weatherford felt that he must enact Dr. Frost's role to his Northern philanthropists and financiers and vicariously make them experience Dr. Peck's conversion to the dream of plenty for mountain folks whose opportunities—physical, intellectual, spiritual—had been so limited.

In his search for money for Berea, Weatherford used the college's Board of Trustees for suggestions and introductions. He drew on his own long acquaintance with funds and their administrators and their varying interests. No lead was too small to follow. An item tucked away in a corner of the New York *Times* could lead him to the offices of a lawyer who had never heard of Berea, but when Weatherford finished telling him of the boys and girls who were educated there he made a four-figure gift to the college and eventually turned over to its trustees the bulk of a small foundation he administered.

Weatherford learned in his fundraising that people are more interested in people than in statistics. He reported to his fellow board members, most of them so-called "hard-headed businessmen" themselves, "Men at these foundations say they give on a scientific basis. Nothing of the kind! They give because you get a man interested in what you're doing and prove to him it's important."

He was well-armed with statistics when he went into conferences. When he had gone to John D. Rockefeller years before asking for money to erect YMCA buildings on college campuses over the South, he had learned that precise figures ("784 students are at this college"—not "about 800") and well-defined goals were necessary to gain attention to a cause. But he learned, too, that it was enthusiasm that raised money. The story at Berea was one of mountain boys and girls, and Weatherford's enthusiasm on that subject was sufficient to the need.

Some brisk secretary might try to discourage his efforts to break the barrier surrounding a prospective friend of Berea, the initial encounter with some icy-countenanced executive who sat down for lunch at the Yale Club might be momentarily difficult, the first refusal from some rich fund whose support had been anticipated might prove disappointing, but such setbacks scarcely shortened Weatherford's stride. He had been in the homes and schools from which Berea's students came. He was fighting for Southern Appalachia's right to survival.

Three months each year were set aside for Weatherford's second task, which was finding prospective students for Berea. This was his labor of love, his fondest commitment. During January, February, and March he went out into the valleys and coves to consolidated schools and one-room schools and all sizes and conditions in between. The first three months of the year were not exactly an ideal season for venturing into the backwoods, but Weatherford went then because those were slack months for raising money. Businessmen were figuring up profits and losses and paying taxes. It was a good time for Weatherford to turn to another sort of investment. Roads were treacherous with snow, rain, ice, mud—but he had discovered that marvelous invention, the jeep, and it opened the winter trails to him.

His goal during these weeks was a visit to four schools each day. When he was able to meet such a schedule, he arrived at the first school by eight o'clock in the morning and left the last school only after it had closed all activities. When he arrived at a high school, he usually addressed the principal as "Professor." Part of Weatherford's method of showing his innate respect for every individual habitually seemed to include this careful awareness of names and titles. He was one of the earliest white leaders in the South to grant Negroes courtesy titles—the simple "Mr." and "Mrs." that seemed to stick in so many polite white throats. Later he did not demean the dignity of boys and girls by calling them "kids" or anything less than a rather formal "young men and women"—which often evoked a response that might be expected of young men and women, as contrasted to kids.

An assembly of the senior class was called and Weatherford spoke to them. They listened. For many of these boys and girls this was the first time anyone had told them they could go to college—if they wanted to badly enough. Many of their own parents had not finished grammar school, a number could not even read or write, and a high school diploma seemed to be a major academic achievement. Now here was someone opening up the possibility of college.

Weatherford frequently told the story of the saddle he had wanted when he was a boy, and bought after years of saving dimes and nickels and quarters. He told them how he had gone to Vanderbilt. Then he told of other boys and girls from places nearby who had determined to win a college education. His call was not for Berea alone but for any school they might want to attend. He was speaking not only to prospective lawyers or doctors but also to those who might farm or work with machinery, and to all of these—especially to those who might become teachers, yes, especially to them—his message was the same: whatever you undertake, do it to the best of your ability and equip yourself with the best possible training.

After his talk, when those seniors who were interested in going on to college met with Weatherford for private interviews, he portrayed college work as being even harder than it was so that those who could be easily discouraged would be promptly discovered. To those who stuck, he opened the gates of Berea and many another college and invited them to learn.

The story of one such boy (whose name will be altered in this account) might stand for numerous similar students and experiences. Weatherford had spoken at a high school in one of the mountain counties of North Carolina. As he talked with the students afterward, a girl asked him, "Why don't you get Luther Hedgepath? He's the best learner we have." Weatherford pounced on the suggestion and sent for Luther, but word came back from his teacher that he wasn't in school that day. "I'll come back and see him later," Weatherford promised. But he didn't mean much later.

The next morning Weatherford appeared at that school again. "Where's Luther Hedgepath?" he asked as he walked into the principal's office. The somewhat startled principal didn't know where Luther was just at that moment but he sent to find out.

When Luther came into the office, Weatherford drew him aside for a long man-to-man talk. At last the boy said, "I'd like to go to college, but I can't. I have to go to work next year and help my mother support all my younger brothers and sisters. It's been enough of a sacrifice for her to get me through high school."

Weatherford took that problem home with him. His conversation with Luther and his teachers and fellow pupils had convinced him this fellow was college material. So he found Luther Hedgepath's mother a job. With this income she was able to support her younger children and release Luther for college.

At Berea, Luther made an excellent record. An inquiry at Berea's office now as to his whereabouts will bring the following reply, "Luther Hedgepath is in California computing data at one of the United States aeronautical space centers. They consider him a valuable man."

There was also the case of Homer Ledford, whose success was different but no less satisfying. After his first three years at Berea, Homer got married. "All he had in the world was a wife," one friend remembers. He went on to a teacher's college at a small town in Kentucky where he taught while he completed his last year of college work. Not long after graduation Weatherford asked him about the carving he had done at Berea. Weatherford admired Homer's dulcimers, replicas of the old musical instruments that the mountain pioneers had played generations before to accompany themselves in the ballads they made up around hearth and bedside. He helped Homer find a market for some of his carefully wrought walnut specimens, and gradually Homer Ledford built up a reputation as one of the finest dulcimer makers in the mountains. At a time when folksongs and handicrafts were having a national revival of popularity, this making of dulcimers became part of a way of making a living as well as part of a way of life.

Wherever he found them, Weatherford took any boy or girl in whom he saw a spark, and he encouraged them. To his disgust he often found them in high schools that were overcrowded, dirty, dilapidated, and run by principals who were little more than educational drones. The atmosphere of such schools reflected the poverty Weatherford was most impatient with: poverty of hope, imagination, or concern. How could children learn or aspire in such an atmosphere, he sometimes asked himself as he bounced along the rutted roads from one school to another. His faithful jeep lived hard at such moments, feeling the tightened grip of his hand on the steering wheel or the emphatic pounding of his hand on the seat as he contemplated the sloth which slowed down progress in the mountains, and as he made up his mind to seek new avenues for rejuvenating the pride of mountain people and bringing them to the attention of the outside world.

In 1953 Weatherford had another big dream. He felt it could be one of the avenues he sought for telling the world and the natives themselves about mountain people. In 1955 Berea would be observing its first centennial. This seemed to Weatherford the perfect occasion for a memorable event which could focus attention not only on Berea but also on all of Southern Appalachia. He went to call on President Hutchins.

"Two years from now Berea will observe its hundredth anniversary," he said. "What are we going to do to celebrate it?"

"I thought we might have some educational conferences," Hutchins replied, "bring in some outstanding men in education and sponsor a series of lectures."

"How much money do you expect to ask us on the Board to vote for this purpose?" Weatherford asked.

"Ten thousand dollars."

"Well, I'll vote for it," Weatherford said. "But then I would like to offer a piece of advice."

Hutchins asked what that would be.

"Take your ten thousand dollars and throw it in a mud hole and go on about your business, for people will forget about lectures in six months."

President Hutchins considered this briefly and then asked, a bit acidly, "Well, what plan do you have?"

He was correct in assuming that Weatherford had a plan. It was to present a drama written by Paul Green in an outdoor theater in the Berea forest that would accommodate fifty thousand people a summer, a drama depicting the struggle of mountain people for education, economic competence, and a more satisfying life. Weatherford stressed the point to Hutchins that Berea had to raise a million dollars a year just to keep going; the wider Berea's story could be known, the easier that task would be.

"And how much will your drama cost?" Hutchins asked.

"$150,000 at least. Maybe $250,000," Weatherford told him. "But I'll raise the money for the theater myself."

When Weatherford presented his proposal at the next meeting of the Board of Trustees, the first member of the Board to speak was a New York lawyer, grandson of a founder of Berea. He favored this drama which could help the mountain people know their own heritage and would also build a constituency of people who knew the college and were informed about its purposes.

There were those on the Board who argued that drama was one of the riskiest of all ventures, however, and they were reluctant to gamble such a heavy investment. After considerable debate, only one member of the Board voted against the motion to let Weatherford proceed with his drama.

Weatherford flew to Chapel Hill, North Carolina, and met Pulitzer prize-winning dramatist Paul Green, who had written the highly successful outdoor pageant *The Lost Colony*. Green had told Weatherford that he couldn't undertake another writing project at that time, but when the older man came in person and told him bits of the story of Kentucky and what he hoped this drama might achieve, the playwright was stirred to acceptance.

By opening night, summer of 1955, some $250,000 had been invested in Green's *Wilderness Road* and in the handsome Indian Fort Theater where it was presented. The theater was located near the site of an old Indian fort three miles from the college campus, and it was built of native stone taken from slave-built fences in the surrounding countryside. The play itself depicted Kentucky's Civil War agony when families, communities, and the state itself were torn asunder. It told the story of a humble man and a dedicated teacher, John Freeman, who gave his life to bring education to the hill country.

Weatherford had reasoned and persuaded where possible, cajoled and bludgeoned where necessary, in bringing together students and faculty, professionals and amateurs, outsiders and villagers, to make *Wilderness Road* a success. He had imbued most of them with his vision of what this drama might accomplish. First, he hoped it would dignify mountain people in the eyes of outsiders by showing them as something other than feuding, moonshine-making illiterates. Second, he felt it could dignify the mountain people in their own eyes by creating a new image for them to live up to. Third, he wanted it to inspire an interest in a college education among mountain boys and girls who otherwise might never consider the possibility. Fourth, he thought it could draw in money for education in the mountains by impressing outsiders with the fact that Southern Appalachia was one of the big wasted resources of this wealthy nation.

Some of Weatherford's hopes were realized that first season. During the first two months of the play's presentation, five hundred more students applied for entrance at Berea alone than had ever done so in a previous season. Favorable reviews given the drama in many of the nation's major newspapers brought the college and the mountain region to the attention of many who were unfamiliar with either.

Wilderness Road ran for four summers. Paid attendance totaled 160,000 during those years. By the fourth year of its presentation, however, it had lost some $25,000 and Berea's Board of Trustees was ready to close it. Some of the members had gone into this project reluctantly, carried along by Weatherford's positiveness and his enthusiasm, and as they had perhaps been oversold at the drama's birth they were now undersold at its demise. Despite Weatherford's efforts to the contrary, *Wilderness Road* was discontinued.

What he had tried to point out to the Board and what he had counted as most important was the fact that returns had accrued to the college through other channels than mere gate receipts to the drama itself. Visitors flocking to attend the drama had brought a boom to the famous college-owned and operated Boone Tavern. The Board of Trustees had spent $500,000 to remodel and modernize the Tavern, and during the two months of July and August in one year gross income reached $117,000 as compared with only $37,000 the previous year.

Sale of crafts made by Berea students showed a similar rise. It increased from $12,000 for the two summer months the first year the drama was presented to $62,000 for the same period during the drama's final season.

In addition, there were at least two large gifts to Berea which were a direct result of *Wilderness Road*. One came from a man in Maryland who set aside $50,000 in his will after reading about the play and the college in a newspaper article. He had never heard of Berea until then. A second bequest came from an elderly woman in Cincinnati. She said she had purposely never visited Berea because she was not in accord with its liberal racial policies, but she had not been able to resist seeing the play and thereby becoming personally acquainted with Berea. She bequeathed the college some $150,000.

A professor of English at Berea College remembers witnessing a brief exchange between playwright Paul Green and one of the men helping stage *Wilderness Road*. He says, "*Wilderness Road* was in rehearsal and one day we heard that Dr. Weatherford had just rescued us from another impasse, accomplished something very important for us, and this man turned to Paul Green who was standing nearby. 'Why does Weatherford put up with it, stay at a little old place like this anyway,' he demanded, 'when he could go on to so many other places?'

"And Green turned on him and said with considerable feeling, 'This is not a little place. It's not a little place because it has big ideas—and big men.'

"We all knew then that Dr. Weatherford had sold Paul Green on his vision of Berea and *Wilderness Road* and the mountain people, too."

The closing of *Wilderness Road* was probably the second keenest disappointment of his career. But he didn't look back. He was too busy looking ahead.

Besides, he could not afford to brood at a time when

his personal life had suddenly had a significant reason for deep joy. Over a period of years he and his wife had almost given up hope that their son would marry. Willis had been good friends with many girls, he had brought several to visit, perhaps he had even been in love, but nothing had ever been mentioned about a wedding. Throughout his life Weatherford had had a special devotion to children, and he had sought out opportunities to be with boys and girls whenever possible. Once he tried to tell Willis what riches a man would miss if he should forego marriage and children, but his son could make small response beyond the private little smile so like his mother's in its affectionate reserve.

Mrs. Weatherford was no less eager than her husband for their son to find the right wife. Willis had made an enviable academic record, balancing a study of religion and economics at the country's best universities. In foreign countries he had worked with practical problems of post-war rehabilitation and village aid. But Julia Weatherford had time to ponder just how lonely the life of a person could be—no matter if he had taken the whole world for his family—if he had no deep personal ties of his own.

Then, in the spring of 1954, when mountain laurel was in pink and white bloom on the mountainside around Far Horizons, Willis brought Anne Smith to visit. Willis was teaching at Swarthmore College where Anne's aunt, Susan Cobbs, was Dean of Women, and Anne was a student. She had been born and reared in Alabama only a few miles from the plantation where Julia McRory had lived, and this link brought Mrs. Weatherford special happiness. When Willis and Anne hiked up one of the trails where so many Blue Ridge visitors had walked in years past and then returned to announce their engagement, Mrs. Weatherford seemed to take on renewed life.

They were married that summer in Greensboro, Alabama, where Anne's family lived, and the Weatherfords could scarcely contain their delight in the quiet, thoughtful brunette Willis had brought into the family. Julia Weatherford wanted to share everything with her, and after each visit from Willis and Anne she would take her wheel chair to closets, shelves, and chests as she divided linens, silver, and treasures Willis had sent from other countries while he was single. With the packages she dispatched to their new home, however, she made it clear to her daughter-in-law that accepting these gifts put under her no obligation to be burdened by them. She could use them or not, give them away if she wished. And, Mrs. Weatherford once pointed out in a wistful effort at lightness, in any event Anne would never have to expect her to be around to "check up" on any of these things. Mrs. Weatherford had learned with her husband, whose life was so filled with purpose and work, and with her son, whose career had taken him around the world, what she was now trying to tell her daughter Anne: that love was a process of letting go, of possessiveness relinquished in the largest generosity of which the human heart was capable.

The following year, in 1955, Willis returned to India and Anne went with him. Mrs. Weatherford dictated a letter to them before their departure. She mentioned the dream she had had many years before. "India has hounded me all my life, for the Foreign Department of the YWCA wanted me to go to India when I first started out in YWCA work but because my father was opposed I did not go but here I find through you that India has finally caught up with me and so it did no good to resist in the first place, I guess."

Her paralysis had reached the point where she had lost all use of her elbows and wrists. She could not even hold the letters from Anne and Willis, which became the brightest spots in her long weeks. When her husband was away a friend—usually Hester Ware, who was an old Blue Ridge P.W.G. whose husband was now executive secrctary and manager of the Blue Ridge Assembly and who lived at the foot of the mountain—read these letters to her. When she replied, Mrs. Weatherford had to dictate. Hester Ware felt the poignancy of such moments when this shy woman could not even communicate with her children except through the medium of a third party. Yet Julia Weatherford remained interested in everything around her—where the cardinals were nesting in a new season, when a friend's baby had been born, the title of a new biography—and she strove to the point of exhaustion to be a gracious hostess. She made house guests as much at ease as possible in the presence of her increasing disability. She directed attention away from herself and thereby made others more relaxed. When Paul Green and his wife, Elizabeth Lay, came to spend a day in late November, 1955, while Green and Weatherford discussed *Wilderness Road* and possible improvements for its second season, Mrs. Green stayed with Mrs. Weatherford in her bedroom, and these two gentlewomen of subtle intelligence had an opportunity to become friends. Mrs. Weatherford felt more a part of the *Wilderness Road* venture after this visit with its rugged, friendly playwright, too.

Before *Wilderness Road* had opened, Paul Green had gone to Berea and spoken to the faculty there about the purposcs of the drama. Some time later Weatherford told President Hutchins that he believed the drama would prove a stimulant, as they intended, to interest in education in the mountains. Now, he wondered, what could be done to improve the quality of religious life in Appalachia?

In 1956, between his forays into the Eastern urban centers for money and his searches for students in the rural county high schools, between work on assembling a staff and actors and promotion for the Berea drama and his duties at Far Horizons, Weatherford approached Hutchins again. "We must do something to awaken the entire nation to Southern Appalachia's needs," he said.

"What did you have in mind?" Hutchins asked. (Perhaps with a slightly patient, faintly wry smile? He had grown somewhat accustomed to asking this question of the man who was now eighty years old but never seemed to run out of ideas.)

Weatherford replied that he would like to call a conference of delegates from all the leading religious denominations represented in the mountains to discuss the situation in Appalachia and to suggest how it might be improved. Weatherford said he would raise the money to finance the conference, and Hutchins gave it his approval.

They stood at the threshold of their largest and most influential enterprise.

17

The offices of that philanthropic Croesus, the Ford Foundation, are at 477 Madison Avenue, New York. They are comfortable but not ostentatious, luxurious without being lavish, and they reflect the likeness of the Foundation to a beneficent but worldly dowager whose acknowledged position of wealth and influence obviates any outward display of either. Carpets are hardly threadbare, yet they are not so deep-piled as to prove embarrassing to visitors unaccustomed to navigating Madison Avenue eyries. Furniture is office modern, not Museum of Modern Art, and the private offices are mere niches compared to some *nouveau riche* spreads along the same street.

Receptionists and secretaries who are buffers between Foundation executives and the public resemble the dowager's deserving grand-nieces—educated, cultivated, pleased to be in her presence. Their employers are the worldly nephews of the dowager—lawyers-on-leave, educators emeritus, social scientists in search of a laboratory, political advisers up from Washington, former executives of industry and the professions—who heeded the rich aunt's call to come and help invest her money in a creative improvement of society.

Paradoxically they must be philosopher-administrators, at once shrewd and naïve, cynical and trusting, simple enough to believe they can effect change and sophisticated enough to be mindful of the proverb that the more things change, the more they remain the same. They are busy contemplators, daydreamers in triplicate who sometimes grow so absorbed in the needs of Humanity that they are deaf to individual human beings abstracted from the one big generalization. There are exceptions. But for the most part these are the administrators of largesse such as ancient Roman emperors or Egyptian queens might have envied, and the responsibility to make wise choices in their Cinderellas is a subtle burden of power. Like the old dowager they represent, they are relaxed in their prestige, strength, resources even as they are most intense in their efforts to broaden and deepen their influence on improving the quality of man's life.

To these offices of quiet power Weatherford laid siege early in 1957. He had come to the Ford Foundation by a route disarming in its directness.

After discussing his conference plans with Berea's President Hutchins, Weatherford had called a five-day interdenominational meeting of religious leaders from Southern Appalachia. Eight denominations sent one hundred delegates to Berea, and these men represented at least 75 per cent of all the church members in the mountain region. Weatherford had assembled a challenging array of speakers, and he arranged for frequent long discussion periods.

By the end of the second day of the conference an informal committee of the delegates came to Weatherford and said they were laboring under a heavy handicap in trying to consider ways to improve the situation in the mountains. Stated briefly, no one knew just what the situation was. There was no source to which they could turn for adequate accurate region-wide data. All of them knew, for instance, that many people were leaving the mountains—but how many? Of what ages? And why?

Weatherford took these men to President Hutchins, and they asked him if he would like to have a region-wide study made with Berea as headquarters. When Hutchins responded enthusiastically, one of the delegates asked if he would give Weatherford time off from his Berea duties and pay his expenses while he explored the possibility of raising funds for such a study. Hutchins agreed.

Weatherford went to work gathering material on the lack of material about the Southern mountains. He discovered that the last survey of the Southern Appalachians had been made in 1932-35 under combined auspices of federal and state government agencies. Even then the facts were based on the 1930 census rather than on any field work.

He acquainted himself with some of the changes transforming the region, and he fortified himself with such statistics and random reports as he could find concerning mountain migrants to the big industrial centers of the nation. (The more he read superficial and sensational journalistic accounts of "hillbilly" invasions of the big cities, the more resolute he became in pushing through a scientific study.)

He approached the Ford Foundation from the top. When he telephoned Henry Heald, the Foundation's president told Weatherford that a group from Central Europe was at that moment in his office and they would not be leaving before five o'clock which was closing time. He would not be in his office the next day, which was Saturday. Weatherford said, "Dr. Heald, if you knew how desperate the situation is in Appalachia I believe you would say 'Come on at five this afternoon, even if it is closing time.' "

"Then come," Heald replied.

Sixty years of training and experience went into the twenty-minute presentation Weatherford made to Heald. Passionate conviction about the worth of the mountain people he represented and the depth of their need tinged his recital of facts and figures and lifted the final summation of his request from the sociological and economic to the moral and spiritual. He had made it a point to be brief—but when he was finished the Foundation president began to ask questions. Weatherford stayed in his office for an hour and a quarter. At the end of that time Heald told Weatherford that he could not speak for the Foundation's Board of Directors but he would be sure that they received a full report of this Appalachian survey request.

In late April, 1957, Weatherford became acquainted with Paul Ylvisaker, director of the public affairs division of the Foundation and a former teaching associate of Weatherford's son at Swarthmore College. The older man was delighted to discover this friend of Willis', and he sensed in Ylvisaker a philosophic depth and sensitive awareness to individuals that would have special meaning in this undertaking to diagram and understand the lives of Southern mountain people. The younger man was impressed by this tough and tender octogenarian who could marshal facts, present them with force, and then illuminate them with anecdotes from his own experience. ("Certain areas in the mountains are industrializing. It's changing our attitudes. A college president in Western North Carolina told me about the mountain man who brought his daughter to the college office and said, 'I brung you my gal and I want you to teach her how to make a living settin' down.' ")

After conversation and correspondence, Ylvisaker summed up his appraisal of Weatherford and his proposal in a memo to an associate. "Mr. Weatherford is a dedicated man, and a hard-headed one. He has spent his life with the mountain people in the South. . . , has the facility of drawing together people, resources and special skills of a very diverse sort, and of bringing them to bear effectively on live problems. Certainly he has done his homework well in this case." He pointed out that it was from the Southern mountains that so many of the in-migrants "to the social abyss of our central cities" were being drawn, and he concluded that a program which would make their point of origin more attractive and more fully equip them for life in the city seemed to make real sense.

A few weeks later Weatherford was back at the Foundation offices talking with another of its executives. His siege was patient and forceful. When this executive made a notation of his meeting with Weatherford, he pointed out to a colleague that "the Appalachian mountain people are the largest and most isolated minority in America, outranking the Indians in both respects." The rest of his report clearly revealed him to be a convert.

When one of the Foundation's representatives went to Berea and journeyed back into the hills to assess some of the existing situation, Weatherford's pet theory about the value of one personal experience or a single human interest story was borne out. When the New York official returned to his offices, he used one encounter he had had in the mountains to illustrate the needs of public health and private attitudes. The incident involved a father who had refused to take a son who had a harelip to the hospital for repair work. The father's argument was that the Lord had made the boy with this handicap and it was not a parent's business to interfere.

The Foundation emissary reported that leaders in the mountains were confident Weatherford could play an important role in mobilizing the support of diverse agencies throughout the area. Among the colleges, religious organizations, and quasi-public bodies, Weatherford's standing was "second to none."

Weatherford himself was busy marshaling support for this survey within the region itself. One of his favorite responses, which he immediately passed along to the Foundation, came from a professor at the University of Tennessee. "The study is timely, in fact it is late."

As he drove forward to keep this work from beginning any later, Weatherford was abruptly halted in mid-passage by a crisis in his personal life. Julia Weatherford suffered a kidney infection in the late summer and a heart attack in September.

For years her condition had been steadily worsening as the paralysis tightened its grip. Weatherford had taken her to a number of doctors and clinics in the South and East. He had bought device after device in an effort to find something which would lessen her dependence on others, give her some degree of mobility. And although at one time she had reached the point of trying to walk with the aid of a walker, the effort had been so demanding and frustrating that her friends had found her with tears flowing down her cheeks as she stood, helpless, in one of her rare displays of emotion.

After slight early improvements, when she had fought for the use of every smallest muscle that would show any sign of response, a slow decline set in. While she could still hold a book, she read widely, sharing the six-thousand-volume library that was the heart of their home. Then this consolation, too, was denied her as she lost control of her arms and fingers.

Aware of the burden an overweight condition would create, she ate sparingly and remained slim. Shampooing and setting her hair, which had grown only slightly grey, was an ordeal but a hairdresser from the village came regularly; she would not give in to sloth and drabness. She dressed, with enormous effort, in soft simple dresses and sweater or stole; when in bed she wore delicate, dressy pink or blue bed jackets. The pink brought out the flush which still tinged her fair skin; the blue accentuated the clear color of her eyes. Her suffering had not left her ravaged—or even aged. And those who saw her after she had undergone the laborious process of being propped in her wheel chair often could not comprehend her complete helplessness.

Her greatest rapport during these years was perhaps with her son. While he was still a young child they had been separated by her long illness and stay in Colorado. Later, they had been separated by the limitation of her paralysis and the natural widening of his interests. But they understood each other with a rare compatibility. After a long absence Willis might come home and a few days after his return a friend would find him in his mother's room, the two of them sitting silently, each radiant in the other's presence, content to share unspoken thoughts.

As for her husband, no one who saw them together could help remarking on the sustained devotion Weatherford accorded his wife, from her most minute wish to her most demanding need. In turn, she spared him all she could when he was home and she remained ready to listen, to applaud or sympathize, at the end of each of his absences as he returned with accounts of the triumphs and defeats he had encountered. She was an excellent listener.

An amusing anecdote she once shared with a close friend revealed a good deal about both of the Weatherfords. During the time when she was still able to ride in the car, Weatherford took her into Asheville one day.

As he parked and went into a store on some errand, he left the car door swinging wide. A passing car struck it and tore the door off its hinges. When Weatherford came back out and saw what had happened, he did not make any comment. Mrs. Weatherford followed suit. They drove home in the somewhat battered car and still neither mentioned the misfortune. The next day he took the car to the garage and had its door replaced and that was that. The episode was closed.

Mrs. Weatherford lived to see one of her five grandchildren, the oldest of the four little girls and boy of Willis and Anne. She had realized her most cherished dream: a full, loving family life for her son.

In September, 1957, after the heart attack, she seemed to rally briefly, and then on the fourth of October she died. She was buried in the little Weatherford Memorial Park area that the Blue Ridge Association had set aside under the avenue of tall white pine sentinels leading down from Lee Hall. An oblong mountain boulder which had required two heavy bulldozers to dislodge and move to this site was marked by a bronze plaque: Weatherford. She was buried on one of the bright October days which sometimes favor the mountains in autumn. Leaves in the woods beyond the dark green pines were turning brilliant red and yellow, the sky was a high blue dome, and the air was so clear that every distant sound seemed to carry across the transparent distance and each peak or valley stood sharply etched in view.

Weatherford knew that his wife's death had been only a release. For the first and only time he spoke of Julia's long trial to his daughter-in-law, Anne. He said that her adversity had revealed the depth of her character. She was a rare soul. And tears flooded his eyes.

A few years later Weatherford made a series of talks to a religious group in which he stressed the power of suffering love. The term as he used it did not define some fleeting romantic indulgence but the most revolutionary allegiance man could grasp. "Suffering love is the greatest transforming power in the world," he said. And although he referred in this statement to historical religious figures and concepts, there is little doubt that his intimate acquaintance with the suffering of one he loved brought a new depth of insight into his understanding and these words.

Once again, in a time of personal pain and loss, Weatherford's belief that "work is a blessing," that "our work is the revelation of our character," was put to test. His grief would have to be borne with the dignity and silent fortitude of a man—and in the meantime, Southern Appalachia was out there waiting, needing.

On November 19, 1957, the Ford Foundation approved a $250,000 grant to Berea College for a survey of the problems of the Southern Appalachian Mountain region and its population.

Weatherford, as Executive Director of the Southern Appalachian Studies, felt that the job now was to choose a team, not just a group of experts.

Presidents of the state universities in the region were contacted, and each of these men gave his consent to a leave of absence for two research men on the faculty in whatever discipline the survey might need. Eventually eleven universities, including all but one of the state universities in the area, several independent colleges, the Tennessee Valley Authority, and some other independent agencies released time for investigators in many fields covered by the survey. The Board of Directors included representatives from fifteen religious denominations and two members from Berea College. Research was begun in June, 1958, under the overall direction of a committee composed of Dr. Earl D. C.

Brewer of Emory University in Atlanta, Dr. Thomas R. Ford of the University of Kentucky, Dr. Rupert B. Vance of the University of North Carolina, and Weatherford.

In February, Weatherford had undergone serious surgery, but by mid-March he was again on the road, coordinating various specialized aspects of the total study. The surgeon was undoubtedly no less relieved than Weatherford when the latter could again be active and follow his full routine of work. When the doctor had first told Weatherford he must allow six weeks for his recuperation, the ramrod-straight gentleman of eighty-two looked him in the eye and said, "I'd like to accommodate you, Doctor, but I can only give you three weeks."

On March 11, 1960, in Greensboro, North Carolina, Weatherford suffered a slight stroke. Little more than two weeks later he was writing to the Ford Foundation people, reporting on the work in progress and making plans for new extensions of the work. No mention was made then or later of any illness on his part. He seemed able to shake off all physical assaults by the strength of interest in his work and his faith in its importance.

Two years later, in 1962, *The Southern Appalachian Region: A Survey,* was published by the University of Kentucky Press. Here was the profile of a forgotten area, the poorest enclave in the wealthiest nation in the world. The survey contained some new and surprising information about the region, confirmed some old fears, and provided an up-to-date background of solid facts by which future plans or administrators could be guided. Governors of the Southern Appalachian states, heads of various public and private agencies, educators and church leaders and officials in Washington, including the President of the United States, had the important material in this volume brought to their attention. It affected momentous decisions they would make for some time to come.

Among the facts which aroused most immediate attention to the 190 Southern Appalachian counties in parts of seven states and some 5½ million people were these:

Between 1950 and 1960, 1,132,000 people migrated from the Southern Appalachians to other areas of the country.

Industrial wages in the area are 20 per cent below the national average.

The farm population is about twice the national average, but many of the farms have a gross income of less than $1,200 a year.

Children attend school an average of 7.2 years, which is 2 years below the national average. Nearly a fifth of the adult population has less than 5 years of schooling.

In the mountain communities, 43 per cent of the ministers have only a twelfth-grade education or less.

There are more churches and smaller churches in the Southern Appalachian counties, but a smaller proportion of the people hold church membership than in the country as a whole. In 1957, for example, 53 per cent of the population of the United States were church members, while only 45.5 per cent of the people of Southern Appalachia belonged to a church.

Numerous other important aspects of the economy, agriculture, local government, attitudes and culture of Appalachia were included in the survey. It accomplished several other goals as well. It clearly defined the size and nature of the problems facing the mountain region. It forced mountain people—including a number of political, educational, religious, and business leaders—to think about mountain problems. Because of the way in which the survey had been initiated, as well as the way it was carried out, several widely divergent, even opposing, groups were brought to cooperate on this common venture. It also helped focus national attention on Appalachia.

One day many months after the Appalachian volume had been published, when the President of the United States and others in Washington were bringing their weight to bear on the problems of the Southern mountains, one of the officials of the Ford Foundation greeted Weatherford in New York with outstretched hands. "Aren't you proud of what you've done? The Southern Appalachian Survey is being discussed all over official Washington. You should devote the next twenty years of your life to this!"

Weatherford smiled with the younger man; he knew something the other didn't. He might not have twenty more years to devote to anything—after all, he was already eighty-seven—but whatever time he did have would be spent—no, more than spent: invested—in Appalachia and its people.

In the survey, the point had been made that what must be developed in Appalachia is not so much the region as the region's people. One of the Ford Foundation's observers of the mountain problems had already recorded his disagreement with many "legislative proposals for assistance to distressed areas, because they assume that 'powdered industry can produce instant jobs,' and they overlook the human resources problem of education and training."

Before the final summary was ever completed, Weatherford had seen a need for deeper understanding and more creative development of Appalachian people. From his experience in efforts to increase understanding between people, he knew that personal contact was most effective. He gave long thought to the hundreds of thousands of migrants, especially those who flocked to the big industrial centers of the Midwest each year, without skills, without knowledge of city life, inviting the disillusionment, even despair, that often awaited them there. He also read colorful newspaper accounts which had appeared in some of those cities, describing hillbilly ghettoes where country music, moonshine whiskey, and mountain justice of knife and knuckle seemed to be the only tangible assets the Appalachian immigrants had brought with them to their urban homes.

Such reports disturbed and angered Weatherford. He knew that qualities of character and habits of behavior which might have been appropriate, even necessary, virtues in a hard, lonely, rural environment, could be anti-social vices in the complex, crowded world of the city. He knew that people—even well-intentioned leaders of social or religious agencies—are often too busy to acquaint themselves thoroughly with specific and apparently difficult groups of strangers, and stereotypes are more easily come by than individualized portraits. And he could not rest until he had made some effort toward lifting the Southern Appalachian people from their stereotypes and revealing them in a dimension he believed to be more truthful.

In the summer of 1958, in conjunction with a workshop on urban adjustment sponsored by the Council of Southern Mountains in Berea, of which Weatherford had long been a member, he took a selected group of thirty-three Midwestern administrators, educators, city and welfare officials on a five-day tour through the heart of Appalachia.

Weatherford rented an air-conditioned bus and took his representatives from seven cities—including Cincinnati, Chicago, Cleveland, and Detroit, chief destinations of so many of the mountain migrants—into the highways and byways of Kentucky, Tennessee, and North Carolina hill country. He was determined to show them a cross section of life in the region, from small mission schools where many boys and girls had received the only education available to them in years past, to giant industries such as the sixty-million-dollar Bowaters paper plant in Calhoun, Tennessee. He pointed out the steep slopes and the narrow creek-bottom farms, coal-mining villages, and agricultural communities, the numerous little churches and the new consolidated schools sprinkled over the countryside. He tried to acquaint these urban people with the deeply rural life most of the mountain people had led until they were plunged into metropolitan, industrial complexes where little of their past experience and few of their customs had any meaning or relevancy. His purpose might have been defined as a missionary effort in reverse, and Weatherford made no effort to conceal his missionary zeal as he preached his message that Southern Appalachian mountaineers were not the dregs of the earth but the deprived of the earth, that they came from a proud heritage which had made its important contribution to the history of America. With some understanding and assistance, he said, they might make yet other contributions in the future.

Such an approach, coupled with Weatherford's almost imperious handling of a group that was more accustomed to administering than being administered, might have been disastrous. Subsequent response indicated that it was eminently successful. Perhaps the comment of a colleague who had helped administer the Southern Appalachian Survey would be applicable in this instance, too: "I saw Weatherford draw together people with widely different ideas of religious doctrine, social science procedures, polity; I saw him deal with the university men, the research specialists and the administrative officials, in the same inclusive way. He could hold their attention and gain their confidence because they respected him. No one could doubt his fairness, his concern, his knowledgeability, and his complete dedication."

As the tour came to a close, Weatherford asked his

guests on the bus that last morning two characteristic questions. "I'm going to ask blunt questions and I want blunt answers," he said. "First, what, if anything, have you learned about the Appalachian people on this trip? Second, what are you going to do about it?"

Results of such people-to-people programs are often difficult to assess. Despite our so-called scientific samplings of opinions and our attitude polls, the individual human mind and collective social atmosphere have not yet yielded to complete documentation. But there were responses to Weatherford's tour that indicated it had made an impression in some of the areas where he felt increased understanding of mountain people was most necessary.

The director of the Department of Welfare in one city returned to his office and had an examination made to determine precisely how many migrants from the Southern Appalachian region were on the so-called relief rolls. To the astonishment of himself and some of his co-workers he discovered the number to be only a fraction of 1 per cent. But he looked at these few with a new awareness, a new empathy.

Answers to Weatherford's questions came in letters throughout the summer. A public school official in Ohio termed the tour a magnificent personal experience and a beneficial professional experience. Weatherford had "opened the door to his background, and bid me see and hear, and climb up the hollows and talk with the mountaineer. How he has hung on so long with so little amazes me. They're hardy folks and though, like everywhere, people come in all kinds, I have gained a respect for and interest in them. Yes, it happened! The enthusiasm of your own keen mind and the overall view of our common problem has rubbed off on me. . . ."

To cite one more response: an official of Illinois' Cook County concluded a two-and-a-half page letter on his trip with the comment that he had enjoyed the tour, but beyond that he felt that it had already accomplished something constructive. Evidence of this could be found in a new and more friendly attitude on the part of some of the Chicago and Ohio press (members of which had been on the trip). He felt that its effect would continue to do good in the future as understanding of mountain people increased.

Weatherford himself subsequently made journeys to some of these cities and became acquainted with a few of the "hillbilly ghettoes." He saw there the worst effects of migration. There were many people, of course, who had gone from the mountains and made the same significant contributions that newcomers from any other region in America might make, but for that large group who were often impelled by desperation alone—hoping to find a subsistence in the city that they had not found in the mountains—conditions were often deplorable. The isolation of their past bred a new isolation in the city. They "belonged" nowhere.

Migration might be the pat answer some people could provide for Appalachia, but Weatherford would not accept it. He knew that it had a sharp cutting edge both for the area the migrants left and for the one to which they went. As one of the writers in the survey had pointed out, migrants from the mountains were usually better educated than the average people they left behind and not so well educated as the average among whom they went to live. A sharp example of this had come to Weatherford's personal attention when he was talking with a teacher in a Kentucky high school. She had told him that not one of her students who had graduated with an A average ten years earlier was still living and working in Kentucky, and not a one with a C average had, so far as she knew, left Kentucky.

The problem, then, was not only to broaden understanding of Appalachian people and their problems outside the region. It was also to deepen understanding of the problems within the region itself. To Weatherford it seemed that a significant place to awaken this understanding was in the churches. Since he was a Methodist he would challenge the second largest denomination in Appalachia to wake up to its backyard needs.

In August, 1962, he called a Southeastern Jurisdictional Council Study Conference and brought together church leaders at Lake Junaluska, North Carolina, the summer assembly center of the Methodist Church. For a week some two hundred and fifty men discussed, learned, and thought about the problems of their region as they had been documented by the Appalachian Survey and developed by Weatherford's probing mind. He spared them no challenge.

"We've thought of the church as a Sunday institution. The community needs us seven days a week.

"Look around you at your region. Because the resources of the mountains are so difficult to develop, these people have had a small measure of material wealth. Hence, they have had low education opportunity and low educational advancement. Too many Americans have therefore jumped to the conclusion that they are a people of low capacity.

"Because the little farms have not given a full task to maintain people, almost all farmers are under-employed. There is not enough opportunity to invest creative labor. This has led the casual visitor to call the highlander a loafer, one who sits on his front porch or on the rail fence and seems to have nothing to do. Let us seek out the real cause of this idleness.

"In the cotton country, 20 acres is the minimum assignment to a Negro man. But in the mountains, $14\,^2/_3$

acres is the maximum average any small farmer can get. What Appalachian people need is more opportunity for creative activity.

"We need new jobs. The income for our region is simply not adequate. And the church must not only teach that 'Man cannot live by bread alone,' it must also admit to its people that 'Man cannot live without bread.'"

He cited the requirements of new industries which would be needed by small county seats, rural communities: water and power—but beyond these, good schools and churches and libraries, all the adjuncts of civilization, too. And whether or not anyone wanted to admit it, it would require federal assistance, too, to lift parts of Appalachia to a level of national equality. "For 25 years we Southern Appalachian people have helped defeat every attempt to lead the nation to lift our educational program where we can have equal opportunity. We started America in order to have a state without privileged classes, but we can never have it until we have access to equal education for all boys and girls. The sooner we wake up, the sooner we will do Christian justice to our boys and girls."

Weatherford's hope and intention was that these church leaders would return to their churches, communities, counties and create a ferment of local change. Many of them never "turned the tap" with the effectiveness Weatherford had wished for. Their conference had achieved one thing, however. It helped create in many areas an informed and concerned nucleus which was needed when the national awareness of Appalachia was aroused and national plans for meeting some of its problems were enacted.

If a precept of Weatherford's had been "do as well as dare, practice as well as preach," he followed his own advice. He set to work on a variety of projects. One involved helping his own community of Black Mountain secure a library. The Appalachian Survey had documented the poverty of cultural experience available in many parts of the region. Weatherford felt that a basic requirement was to make books readily accessible to anyone who wanted them.

A library committee was formed and began to look around for an appropriate site in Black Mountain. A downtown lot situated beside one of the banks seemed an ideal location. The bank was approached and after considering the matter offered the library an area 70 feet wide and 110 feet deep. Weatherford politely declined. It did not allow enough room for any initial spaciousness or any subsequent growth. Finally the size of the lot was increased to 80 feet by 160 feet and the Black Mountain Friends of the Library accepted the gift. Asheville architects drew up plans for the modern, one-story structure. When the task of raising $55,000 (to be matched by $55,000 of federal funds) was begun in the summer of 1965, Weatherford told the Friends of the Library it was the biggest job "we've ever faced for the whole town of Black Mountain." Then he added, "Nothing is more important than giving something to help young people become better citizens."

The state librarian came up to the mountain town to discuss the new concept of the modern library with its open areas, rugs and easy chairs and easily accessible books, special children's room, conference and exhibition areas, rooms for showing films and holding public discussions. Weatherford went after the larger donations— and he worked no less eagerly for this little library than he had for much larger buildings a half-century or quarter of a century earlier.

A journalist writing in *Reporter* magazine a few months before Weatherford and the library committee had begun its formal drive observed, "One of Appalachia's problems is the inability of counties and cities to raise the usual local share necessary to obtain Federal matching funds for such things as airports, hospitals, vocational education facilities, libraries, and flood control." The inability of some counties and cities to raise their share of funds is sometimes due to lack of local leadership as well as lack of money, however. The success of Weatherford and his Friends of the Library proved this point as construction began on the library they had worked so hard to achieve.

When he advised the Methodist preachers to tell their mountain people that bread alone is not enough but bread itself is essential, he knew that he was touching on one of the deepest dilemmas of mountain life: how to make a living in the modern world without forfeiting all the old values and traditions. When he tried to think of specific ways in which he could help some of those people who persisted in living back in the landlocked coves, he came up with another project.

He looked out at the mountains opposite his home and thought of that tallest pinnacle, Mt. Mitchell, which was now a state park, visited by thousands of people each year as they turned off the Blue Ridge Parkway and took a spur road to climb the highest mountain in the East. He went to visit the building the state had erected at the parking space just below the summit of Mt. Mitchell. The largest room was a lounge with a few seats and a big picture window framing a magnificent view. Weatherford visited that lounge several times. He sat at one side and watched visitors as they came and went. On his large gold pocket watch he timed one hundred of these people and found that they spent an average of twenty seconds each in contemplating the view. Surely such a heavily visited spot could be put to more meaningful use.

Weatherford went to see North Carolina's Governor

Terry Sanford and told him of his survey of man-hour (or man-seconds) enjoyment of the Mt. Mitchell lounge. Then he proposed that the state turn this room into a craft shop where the native handwork of the mountain people could be displayed and sold. When the state agreed to this, Weatherford approached the newly formed Area Redevelopment Administration in Washington and asked for capital to start a craft shop.

"I want to prove two things," he said. "First, that we can find crafts deep in these Appalachian mountains that deserve to be sold to a discriminating public. Second, that people will buy enough of these native crafts to keep such a shop in business."

The ARA approved the plan and provided the capital, and Weatherford found two knowledgeable persons with long experience in the mountains in judging and selling handcrafts. They bounced up mountain roads and down rough little valleys searching out people with talent in their fingers and need at the door. They found plenty of each. Within two seasons the more or less empty lounge at Mt. Mitchell had been transformed into a beautiful and useful showcase for at least a handful of the mountain people. Some two hundred and twenty-five families were receiving a little more cash than they had had before. Beyond the cash, it seemed to Weatherford that this and all the other similar handcraft showcases scattered through the region could enlarge national appreciation of the mountain people. How could anyone look at a piece of delicate and intricate handweaving, hold a beautifully designed piece of pottery, contemplate an imaginative carving in rich walnut or cherry, and not realize that people who could create such objects were worthy of attention, of approval, of assistance if necessary.

Weatherford was not naïve enough to believe that a library in one community, a craft shop in one state park would turn the tide of fortune in Appalachia. But perhaps it is a reverse sort of naïveté which says that since one man cannot accomplish everything he should attempt nothing. The meaning of Weatherford's life and of his prophecy of plenty is implicit in his specific local endeavors no less than in his large, more universal visions. He has managed to combine the homely dictum of his old friend, Booker T. Washington, "Let down your bucket where you are," with the austere magnificence of Pierre Teilhard de Chardin, whose thought he has absorbed: "In action I cleave to the creative power of God. I coincide, I become not only its instrument but the living prolongation . . . . The soul is wedded to a creative effort."

Whatever Weatherford has undertaken quickens to life because it involves people. For him the Southern Appalachian Survey was not a book of dry statistics, bloodless polls, and paper plans. It was the story, in broad and factual terms, of men and women, boys and girls he had been encountering up and down the hills and hollows, in the towns and crossroads of Appalachia for many decades.

If the Ford Foundation people who had furnished the funds to bring this report to its fruition would not soon forget W. D. Weatherford, neither would many other people scattered through the mountains who had unwittingly provided the pity, dismay, hope which were the seeds of such a survey.

There was the boy in Kentucky who didn't know the name of the river in the town where he lived. "Why don't you learn it?" Weatherford had challenged him. "You're poor and you'll always be poor as long as you're ignorant. Learn the name of that river at least! And the next fact you learn will come even easier."

There was a high-school-age filling station attendant at a town named Sevierville, near Tennessee's Great

Smoky Mountains. When Weatherford stopped to buy some gas and asked him where the town got its name, "Did John Sevier ever live here?" the boy only replied, "Hunh? Who?"

"Can it be possible," Weatherford said, "that you have lived here all your life and you don't know who John Sevier was?"

"Never heered of him," the attendant muttered.

"Well, I've been buying gas here for years," Weatherford said, "as I travel back and forth through the mountains, but I'll never buy another gallon till you know who John Sevier is."

The following summer when Weatherford pulled into the station, the same fellow came out, took his hose off the gas pump, and approached Weatherford's car. "Hold on! I'm the man who wants to know who John Sevier was."

A grin both sheepish and triumphant broke over the boy's face. He told Weatherford about John Sevier, pioneer settler and first governor of his state. "He'd learned!" Weatherford concluded as triumphantly as if he'd won a great contest.

There was the Indian boy Weatherford sought out when one of the women buying for the Mt. Mitchell craft shop had returned with a bear and an owl the twelve-year-old had carved. Weatherford drove over a hundred miles and when he came to Jimmy's house up one of the narrow coves on the Qualla Reservation, he found an authentic Cherokee family—reserved, bright-eyed, attentive. Jimmy's mother and brown-eyed brothers and sisters listened as he praised the boy's present work and suggested how it might be made even better in the future. He encouraged him to do special carvings of the black bears native to the mountains. And then, as he made ready to leave the little cabin, wondering if he had made any impression on this reticent household, a seven-year-old brother standing to one side looked Weatherford straight in the eye and said, "When I grow up, I'm going to carve a better bear than Jimmy ever made!"

To Weatherford this seemed the very best spirit of Appalachia speaking. This was the voice of the sturdy old ancestors whose determination he had seen in his own mother's face. This was the indomitable self-reliance and search for progress that had been the theme of *Wilderness Road*. This was the voice of youth he had searched out for Berea and a dozen other colleges through many winters, for which the Appalachian Survey had been made.

There were others, of which the ones described were probably only the least. Archibald MacLeish in his book *The Eleanor Roosevelt Story* made an observation which also applies to the Weatherford story: "People were everything to her; not only her own people but all the others everywhere. And it is largely for this reason that her understanding of her own time . . . seems sounder in retrospect than the understanding of many of her husband's best-informed advisers. They thought in terms of policies; she thought in terms of people."

18

One day while the Weatherfords were still dividing their life between Nashville, Tennessee, and the mountains of Western North Carolina, Rosa Lea McKesson assured a visitor to Blue Ridge: "Dr. Weatherford runs this place by grit and grace and greenbacks."

Dr. Alexander Heard, brilliant young chancellor of Vanderbilt University, said much the same thing but more formally when he wrote the present director of Blue Ridge, on the occasion of Weatherford's ninetieth birthday, in 1965: "His career has been as courageous and creative as it has been long. His lifetime of labor for social justice, wider economic horizons, and better conditions of life for the people of our section has won enduring fame for him and lasting pride for his alma mater."

Although they could rejoice in his achievements after they had been won, there were those among Weatherford's associates through the years who were left somewhat breathless at the daring and rapidity with which his dreams multiplied. They may have felt toward him much as George MacDonald, the Scottish preacher, regarded a Higher Being: "God is often pleased but never satisfied."

With each new accomplishment Weatherford seemed to discover new challenges. The tasks and travels of his life overlapped ever more intensely. While he was building Blue Ridge Assembly he was also traveling—to Europe, to Korea, to Japan, to China—speaking sometimes three and four times a day, and at the same time enlarging his own knowledge, experience, and wisdom. While he was working to secure attention and information for the Appalachian mountain region he was also writing a book called *American Churches and the Negro* (published in 1957), which provided historical precedent and religious pressure for church leadership in bringing justice to black-white relationships. And while he was writing *Pioneers of Destiny*, a paean of praise to the character of the Scotch-Irish settlers of the mountains (published in 1955), and while he was co-authoring a study of *Life and Religion in Southern Appalachia* (published in 1962), he was also politicking with governors, preaching to ministers, educating teachers, selling businessmen on the potential which often seemed buried under the problems of Appalachia.

"Weatherford," a friend once remarked, "will be remembered not by what he possessed but by what possessed him."

And the chief conviction which has possessed him and still does is that the proper study of mankind is man: the proper concern of humanity is human beings.

The impact of Weatherford's life as he has been guided, forged, refined by the fires of that conviction cannot be measured by any seismograph or slide-rule. There are many obvious reasons for this—one of the chief ones being that that influence is not yet accomplished, complete. It continues. For the initial commitment of Weatherford's life is only today coming into the fullest public attention: knowledge that there is a cancerous poverty in our midst, and poverty in any segment of our lives diminishes the possibility of true plenty everywhere.

What is poverty? Poverty is lack of physical necessities, lag of intellectual development, loss of spiritual passion.

And what is plenty? Plenty is adequacy to meet the body's needs, energy to spark the mind's thrust outward, vision to behold the spirit of man as it struggles upward.

A prophecy of plenty appears to be the very latest innovation on our mid-twentieth century social scene. Erich Fromm the psychologist has recently written: "The shift from a psychology of scarcity to that of abundance is one of the most important steps in human development. A psychology of scarcity produces anxiety, envy, egotism (to be seen most drastically in peasant cultures all over the world). A psychology of abundance produces initiative, faith in life, solidarity."

W. D. Weatherford was prophesying and practicing this psychology of abundance half a century ago. His life testifies to the accuracy of Fromm's statement that such a psychology produces initiative, faith in life, solidarity.

When Weatherford began his career he embraced this sense of prophecy in the terms described by a thoughtful young theologian who created quite a stir late in 1964 with some observations on preaching, in which he said, among other things, "Genuine preaching originates in the prophetic impulse, which is like the impulse to art, or science, or philosophy. Preaching of this kind has a place if it makes a place, but its place is not assured. Preaching that is modeled on the prophetic ideal will evoke our ultimate concern. [Such preaching and prophecy] is devouring and bears down a man's energies and emotions, and like every other job, in one way or another, it will cost a man his life."

Seventy years later, that prophetic impulse still bears down on Weatherford's energies and emotions as it did when he was twenty. In some ways, as Dr. Benjamin Mays, President of Morehouse College, has remarked, Weatherford seems to have reversed the usual aging process in which the pattern is one of liberal impatience during youth and a more weary wariness of later years. Weatherford seems never to have been weary, but he was in some ways more wary when he was young than now, when years have increased his liberalism—and his impatience. His close friend, President Hutchins of Berea, says "Weatherford has had more imaginative ideas since he was eighty than most men have in a lifetime!"

The past decade brought a harvest of honors: LL.D. degrees from Berea College and the University of North Carolina at Chapel Hill; convocations at Blue Ridge's 50th Anniversary; and 80th, 85th, 90th birthday tributes from around the world; a nation-wide citation from the National Council of Churches for contribution to rural life. Yet even as these and other recognitions came for work done yesterday, Weatherford was already facing up to tomorrow.

On December 1, 1965, the Appalachian Regional Commission in Washington formulated a resolution congratulating Weatherford on his 90 years, citing his "lifetime of service to the mountain people" and his administration of the "outstanding survey, *The Southern Appalachian Region.*" It pointed out that "his ideas, his energy and his leadership have greatly aided in focusing national concern and attention on the region which now has been translated into action in the Appalachian Regional Development Act of 1965 and this Commission's current program to develop the Appalachian Region."

But including and beyond Appalachia, Weatherford had caught a vision of the new society opening to man.

It is not a society brought about by political decree or the definitions of any single academic discipline, but by changes so numerous and so basic to our lives that only our most advanced thinkers have begun to state and correlate and judge them and bring them to our faltering attention.

One of the consistently remarkable facts of Weatherford's life has been his ability to take the parts and see a whole, study the evidence of today and discern the shape of tomorrow. This has resulted not from any magical powers but from a willingness to look deep and see, listen patiently and hear, feel keenly—and think.

By this method he realized early in the century that the South and nation would never achieve true health until the question of race had been squarely faced and justly settled.

Equally as early he advocated that education would be the lever which could loosen the grip of poverty, but that education had to be shaped to one standard: excellence.

Then he understood that Appalachia and all that it represented must confront the conscience of the country, not only for what it was but also for what it could be. "The elemental need," he said over and over, "is to give new hope and new appreciation for his own worth and dignity to the mountain man—to all men."

Future historians must assign Weatherford his niche in history (although it may be difficult to confine him to a mere niche). They may also puzzle at some length over the precise category which will describe him: liberal? radical? moderate? conservative? At various periods, under various circumstances, he was each of these —sometimes two or three at the same time. He might adopt an idea that was radical for his time and place— and then employ moderate, indeed conservative, means to bring the idea to general attention and eventual acceptance. His purpose was to win the ultimate goal, not to pursue either boldness or caution for its own sake. Labels and categories were not his concern; he was occupied with constructive change and growth.

To some extent, the combination of his unusual idealism buttressed by a hard-headed pragmatism reflected the influence of his rural nineteenth-century South-western boyhood. Religion and family ties and familiarity with the natural world all helped to foster his innately idealistic and affirmative approach to life. At the same time, no one could survive on a farm—putting forth hard work, enduring the destructive or helpful whims of weather—without becoming something of a pragmatist, a realist. As these two attitudes met and merged in Weatherford's life and work, they made it possible for him to labor with many different types of people and reconcile them to each other and to the future. Historians will have to decide whether a man who believes in the sacredness of persons and makes this the basis of his life and work is a radical departing from the traditions of Jefferson, Madison, and other great Southern Americans, or whether he is a true conservative of the South's and the nation's most basic values.

And along the way he began to grapple with another realization: that of the new industrial revolution of cybernetics which is transforming our world and pushing us down the path of unprecedented social change. To analyze that change and direct it, mold it to the needs of men rather than forfeit it to the whims of chance, Weatherford feels we must pay it more than marginal attention. Our best effort must be turned to survival — survival of the spirit even as others plot our physical survival in the day of the H-bomb.

"We must get interested in producing better people instead of more things." That is Weatherford's summons —and it is a call to revolution. Its implications, if considered even for a moment, shake every institution in our society. At a time when the prosperity of our technology commands us, "Produce! Consume!" Weatherford bids us, "Create!"

What does such a shift from pure consumer to partial creator mean? What are the implications of turning from a smooth and standardized production to the rough trial-and-error of individual creation? The meaning and implication calls for a revised definition of religion—larger, tougher, richer than the doctrine which now permits division of life into the sacred and the secular. It calls for a new definition of work.

Weatherford is not afraid to stand in that lonely place where his thought and his faith lead him. He does not quake before the realization that we must make a massive investment in people. He is not afraid to say that the time has come when it is as important to repair a broken man as a broken computer. In redefining work he is not afraid to suggest that it is as important to pay a boy's keep in school before he has gotten into trouble as to pay his keep in prison after he has made trouble, or to suggest that erosion of a man's dignity is at least as important as the erosion of his cornfield.

In the summer of 1964 Weatherford set down some thoughts on the situation in Appalachia which had broad implications for man's general situation: "There is no easy answer. Each person must have a living wage. But how can we give that money and still maintain the self-respect, the individuality and dignity of the recipients?

"I suggest that every person who draws material aid shall be made to feel that he must render an equivalent return to society, not in material goods produced because he has no job where material goods can be produced, but in values which society needs and must have, such as educational values, motivational values, spiritual values, service values, which society must have to reach its highest culture.

"The educational and spiritual institutions of society must impress on all recipients of necessary aid that it is a debt of honor which they owe society and they are duty bound to pay. And these spiritual and educational institutions must work out some sane and practical ways in which such a debt may be discharged. Anything less than this will destroy the self-respect of the recipient. Such a solution as this would tax our spiritual resources to the limit, but if fulfilled it might mean a new life for the church and education, and the transformation of society itself."

Thus he gives the church a challenge to be central to man's life once more. He does not believe that God is dead—but the church may be dead if it is only an institution of bricks and budgets. The church as a living prophecy could revive Appalachia—and the world.

If much of Weatherford's life was devoted to combating a narrow, primitive fundamentalism which would reduce religion to some rigid system of rote and score-keeping by which winners achieve heaven hereafter and losers wind up in eternal torment, so his thrust today is against a specious intellectualism and an enervated liberalism which would render religion impotent in its influence on the daily pressures and realities of life.

It is difficult to escape the conclusion that Weatherford's proposals concerning specific problems of Appalachia and of modern man in general gain less attention than they merit because they are religiously motivated. Our society may be verbally committed to its official Christianity, but at its sources of power it is deeply suspicious of any proposals based primarily on Christianity's principles. In discussion of the social revolution bearing down upon us, he who provides an economist's analysis, a sociologist's study, a politician's blueprint wins at least momentary attention and respect. But he who sets forth the liberal religious statesman's thought often walks alone—even among the church hierarchy. "Far Horizons" was not built, however, by a man who could not bear loneliness. Once, when asked how he met criticism over the years, he replied, "I just keep on rowing and don't rock the boat." And so Weatherford works now on some plan, some *modus vivendi* by which he can move the church—in Appalachia, in America—closer to both man and God.

"Oh no!" a young political "realist" groaned recently when told of Weatherford's latest concerns and his hope for the church. "Let's just let that obsolete institution R.I.P. under its headstone—we've too much to do to wait for it to move!"

The sophisticated and knowledgeable administrators and functionaries of philanthropic giants in urban centers across the country murmur restively at such an innocuous word as "spiritual" and such a controversial term as "religious." Their actions speak loudly: "Poverty of body—show us the slums, the run-down farms, the dilapidated hospitals—with this we can work. Poverty of mind—enrichment programs in the schools? preschools?—this we can consider. Poverty of spirit—whose spirit? what is the geography of a soul?—this we must leave to someone else." And again the sacred and the secular are divided, and man's work remains essentially without integration.

But the old man who is tough as mountain oak sweeps winter snow off of his balcony porch at "Far Horizons" and walks the length of it back and forth, back and forth, thinking, thinking. "That porch is thirty-three feet long," he says, "and if I walk it one hundred times I do almost three-fifths of a mile. I try to make it every night I'm home."

The valley lies far below him; lights winding along

the length of the interstate highway flicker like fireflies. But beyond and opposite him loom the craggy mountains, their shapes dark in the night but the paths to each of their pinnacles known and tested by Weatherford's feet in years past. Between the valley and the peaks he paces sturdily, thinking, planning, dreaming. He knows that the adventure between man and man, between man and God, is born neither of the jungle nor of myth but is the only dream worthy of reality.

"When I work with human beings anywhere if I work in the spirit of good will and understanding I will find personal growth toward God as in no other way. This gives what Teilhard de Chardin calls a passionate faith in the purpose and splendor of human aspiration and that becomes the flame which illumines all our efforts.

"I believe most people who fail do fail because either they cannot dream or if they dream their dreams are too small. The bolder our dreams for the welfare of our fellow men the more likely it is that humanity will see the meaning of our dreams and help to bring them to reality. Most of all I believe that the scope of a man's dreams is the measure of his faith in God and his belief in his fellow men.

"I would paraphrase a familiar quotation and say, Be bold when you dream of the kingdom of God and the welfare of your fellow man, and the courage that lies in others sleeping but never dead will rise and dare to help make your dreams come true."

The road which began ninety years ago in a log cabin on the plains of Texas led to the summit of "Far Horizons" in North Carolina's mountains. And all along the way there has been a goodly company, those who discovered and dispensed a new plenteousness of body, mind, and spirit because they had encountered its prophecy in W. D. Weatherford.

ACKNOWLEDGMENTS

If W. D. Weatherford, his life, and its meaning, come alive in this book, part of the credit must be shared with those who helped me so generously. Sometimes they gave me hours of their time and the riches of years of memory. Sometimes they provided me with but a single insight or a moment's vignette. In either case, they were helpful. The names of those I acknowledge below form an incomplete list, but they are the ones to whom I am most immediately and deeply grateful. None of them, of course, is responsible for errors of omission or commission in this book.

There are several groups of people who were cordial in assisting my research. These include officials of the American Cast Iron Pipe Company in Birmingham, Alabama; officials of the Southeastern YMCA; administration and faculty of Berea College in Berea, Kentucky; leaders of various religious denominations throughout the South; Ford Foundation executives.

The assistance of W. D. Weatherford, Jr., and his wife Anne has been an adventure in friendship as well as in scholarship. Their modesty may have hindered research occasionally but their achievements have brought only honor to their father, to themselves, and to their country.

Among others who have made a real contribution are Agnes Highsmith Ware, Dr. Frank Graham, Mr. and Mrs. Henry Ware, Mr. and Mrs. Robert Eleazer, Mrs. Charles Johnson (before her death), Patricia Johnson Clifford, Elizabeth Wyckoff, Dorothy Burgess, Carlton Parker, Frances Eleazer Schneider, Dr. William H. Morgan and Dr. Mildred Morgan, Mrs. Susan Young Eagan, Eugene Barnett, Charles L. Wharton, Dr. A. B. Cash, Dr. James Sells, Thomas M. Kreider, Jerome W. Hughes, Miss Elizabeth Gilbert of the Berea Library, President Francis Hutchins of Berea, Emily Ann Smith, Charity Cummingore, Dr. Elisabeth Peck, Paul Green, Kenneth Daniel, Allen Post, Dr. O. C. Carmichael, Paul Ylvisaker, Dr. Paul Limbert, John R. Poteat, J. W. MacKay, Dr. Benjamin Mays, Dr. John Hope Franklin, Dr. B. Z. Welch, Loyal Jones, Howard Kester, Ralph Frost, John Hampton, Hiden Ramsey, Rupert Vance, Billy Edd Wheeler, Percy Ferrebee, and George M. Stephens.

BOOKS BY W. D. WEATHERFORD

(LISTED IN ORDER OF DATE OF PUBLICATION)

Fundamental Religious Principles in Browning's Poetry. Nashville: Publishing House of the M. E. Church, South, 1907.

College Problems. Vols. 1–3. Nashville: Publishing House of the M. E. Church, South, 1907, 1908, 1909.

Negro Life in the South. New York: Association Press, 1910.

Introducing Men to Christ. Nashville: Publishing House of the M. E. Church, South, 1911.

Present Forces in Negro Progress. New York: Association Press, 1912.

Personal Elements in Religious Life. Nashville: Publishing House of the M. E. Church, South, 1916.

Christian Life a Normal Experience. New York: Association Press, 1916.

The Negro from Africa to America. New York: Doran Co., 1924.

Survey of the Negro Boy in Nashville 1932. Edited by WEATHERFORD. New York: Association Press, 1932.

Race Relations. (With CHARLES S. JOHNSON.) Boston: D. C. Heath & Co., 1934.

James Dunwoody B. De Bow. Southern Sketches, No. 3. Charlottesville, Va.: The Historical Publishing Co., Inc., 1935.

Analytical Index of De Bow's Review. Santa Barbara, Cal.: Privately published, 1948.

Religion in the Appalachian Mountains. A Symposium. Edited by WEATHERFORD. Berea, Ky.: Berea College Press, 1955.

Educational Opportunities in the Appalachian Mountains. Edited by WEATHERFORD. Berea, Ky.: Berea College Press, 1955.

Pioneers of Destiny. Birmingham: Vulcan Press, 1955.

American Churches and the Negro. Boston: Christopher Publishing House, 1957.

Life and Religion in Southern Appalachia. (With EARL D. C. BREWER.) New York: Friendship Press, 1962.

The Southern Appalachian Region: A Survey. Edited by Thomas R. Ford; Weatherford, Director of Research. Lexington: University of Kentucky Press, 1962.

Studies in Christian Experience. Nashville: Methodist Evangelistic Material, 1962.

RELATED READINGS

Like Caesar's Gaul, W. D. Weatherford's life has been divided into three parts. His work in each of these three fields of major concern has overlapped, of course, but generally speaking the first part of his career emphasized education and race relations while the later years brought a concentration on the people of the Southern Appalachians. Religious concern informed each undertaking.

It has seemed, therefore, that this bibliography might be most clear and useful if it were divided into at least two major categories. Part I includes those books, pamphlets, and periodicals that either are directly relevant to Weatherford's own life or provide special insight into the first two fields of his interests: education and Negro-white relationships. Part II of the bibliography includes those publications which are useful in understanding or interpreting Weatherford's work with reference to the mountain region.

Part I: Books Related to Weatherford's Life

Agee, James, and Walker Evans. *Let Us Now Praise Famous Men.* Boston: Houghton Mifflin Co., 1941.

Ashmore, Harry S. *The Negro and the Schools.* Chapel Hill: University of North Carolina Press, 1954.

Association Men. YMCA Magazine. Discussions of Blue Ridge Assembly, October 1910, October 1917, October 1925.

Augsburg, Paul D. *Bob and Alf Taylor.* Morristown: Tennessee Book Co., 1925.

Baker, Ray Stannard. *Following the Color Line.* New York: Doubleday, Page and Co., 1908. Reissued in 1964 by Harper & Row Torchbooks, New York, with an Introduction by Dewey W. Grantham.

BARDOLPH, RICHARD. *The Negro Vanguard*. New York: Rinehart and Co., 1959.

BIZZELL, WILLIAM B. *Rural Texas*. New York: Macmillan Co., 1924.

Blue Ridge Voice. Publication of the Blue Ridge Assembly. Issues from November 1919 to June 1927.

BOND, HORACE MANN. *The Education of the Negro in the American Social Order*. New York: Prentice-Hall, Inc., 1934.

BONTEMPS, ARNA. *Story of the Negro*. New York: Alfred A. Knopf, 1951.

———. *100 Years of Negro Freedom*. New York: Dodd, Mead and Co., 1961.

BROWN, INA CORINNE. *Race Relations in a Democracy*. New York: Harper & Bros., 1949.

CARROLL, CHARLES. *The Negro a Beast*. St. Louis: American Book & Bible House, 1900. (This is an example of the horror literature that was peddled through the South during the early part of the century. Its title page carried a summation of its theme: "The Negro a beast, but created with articulate speech, and hands, that he may be of service to his master—the White man.")

CARTER, HODDING. *Southern Legacy*. Baton Rouge: Louisiana State University Press, 1950.

CASH, W. J. *The Mind of the South*. New York: Alfred A. Knopf, 1941.

CASON, CLARENCE. *90° in the Shade*. Chapel Hill: University of North Carolina Press, 1935.

CLARK, THOMAS D. *The Emerging South*. New York: Oxford University Press, 1961.

CLIFT, VIRGIL A., ARCHIBALD W. ANDERSON, and H. GORDON HULLFISH, editors. *Negro Education in America*. New York: Harper & Row, 1962.

COHN, DAVID L. *The Life and Times of King Cotton*. New York: Oxford University Press, 1956.

COLBERG, MARSHALL RUDOLPH. *Human Capital in Southern Development, 1939–1963*. Chapel Hill: University of North Carolina Press, 1965.

COMMISSION ON INTERRACIAL COOPERATION. *America's Tenth Man*. Atlanta, 1930.

———. *The Mob Still Rides*. Atlanta, 1936.

———. *The Interracial Commission Comes of Age*. Atlanta, 1942.

CULVER, DWIGHT W. *Negro Segregation in the Methodist Church*. New Haven: Yale University Press, 1953.

DABBS, JAMES MCBRIDE. *The Southern Heritage.* New York: Alfred A. Knopf, 1958.

DABNEY, CHARLES WILLIAM. *The General Education Board: An Account of its Activities, 1902–1914.* New York: General Education Board, 1915.

——. *The Southern Education Movement.* Chapel Hill: University of North Carolina Press, 1936.

——. *Universal Education in the South.* 2 vols. Chapel Hill: University of North Carolina Press, 1936.

DABNEY, VIRGINIUS. *Liberalism in the South.* Chapel Hill: University of North Carolina Press, 1932.

DICKEY, J. A., and E. C. BRANSON. "How Farm Tenants Live." *University of North Carolina Extension Bulletin.* Vol. ii, No. 6, November 16, 1922.

DOBIE, J. FRANK. *The Flavor of Texas.* Dallas: Dealey and Lowe, 1936.

DOWD, JEROME. *The Negro in American Life.* New York: Century Co., 1926.

DOYLE, BERTRAM W. *The Etiquette of Race Relations in the South.* Chicago: University of Chicago Press, 1937.

DUBOIS, W. E. B. *Darkwater: Voices from the Veil.* New York: Harcourt, Brace and Co., 1920.

——. *Black Folk, Then and Now.* New York: Henry Holt & Co., 1939.

——. *The Souls of Black Folk.* Chicago: McClurg & Co., 1903.

DYKEMAN, WILMA, and JAMES STOKELY. *Neither Black nor White.* New York: Rinehart and Co., 1957.

——. *Seeds of Southern Change: The Life of Will Alexander.* Chicago: University of Chicago Press, 1962.

ELEAZER, ROBERT B. *A Realistic Approach to the Race Problem.* Atlanta: Commission on Interracial Cooperation, 1939.

EMBREE, E. R. *Brown America.* New York: Viking Press, 1931.

FRANKLIN, JOHN HOPE. *From Slavery to Freedom.* New York: Alfred A. Knopf, 1947.

FRAZIER, E. FRANKLIN. *The Negro Family in the United States.* Chicago: University of Chicago Press, 1939.

——. *The Negro Church in America.* New York: Schocken Books, 1963.

GRANT, MADISON. *The Passing of the Great White Race; or, the Racial Basis of European History.* New York: Charles Scribner's Sons, 1916.

GRANTHAM, DEWEY W., JR. *The Democratic South.* Athens: University of Georgia Press, 1963.